W9-BCS-082

Sexuality and Teens

*What You Should Know About Sex,
Abstinence, Birth Control,
Pregnancy, and STDs*

AUSTIN PUBLIC LIBRARY

Sexuality and Teens

What You Should Know About Sex, Abstinence, Birth Control, Pregnancy, and STDs

ISSUES IN FOCUS TODAY

Stephen Feinstein

Enslow Publishers, Inc.
40 Industrial Road
Box 398
Berkeley Heights, NJ 07922
USA

http://www.enslow.com

Copyright © 2010 by Stephen Feinstein

All rights reserved.

No part of this book may be reproduced by any means
without the written permission of the publisher.

Library of Congress Cataloging-in-Publication Data

Feinstein, Stephen.
    Sexuality and teens : what you should know about sex, abstinence, birth control,
pregnancy, and stds / Stephen Feinstein.
        p. cm.
    Includes bibliographical references and index.
    Summary: "Discusses sexuality and teens, including teen sex, abstinence, birth
control, teen pregnancy, sexually transmitted diseases, and sex education in schools"
—Provided by publisher.
    ISBN-13: 978-0-7660-3312-2
    ISBN-10: 0-7660-3312-0
    1. Teenagers—Sexual behavior—Juvenile literature. 2. Sex customs—Juvenile
literature. I. Title.
    HQ27.F45 2010
    306.70835—dc22
                                    2009001373

032010 Lake Book Manufacturing, Inc., Melrose Park, IL

Printed in the United States of America

10 9 8 7 6 5 4 3 2

To Our Readers: We have done our best to make sure all Internet addresses in this book were
active and appropriate when we went to press. However, the author and the publisher have no
control over and assume no liability for the material available on those Internet sites or on
other Web sites they may link to. Any comments or suggestions can be sent by e-mail to com-
ments@enslow.com or to the address on the back cover.

♻ Enslow Publishers, Inc., is committed to printing our books on recycled paper. The paper in
every book contains 10% to 30% post-consumer waste (PCW). The cover board on the outside
of each book contains 100% PCW. Our goal is to do our part to help young people and the envi-
ronment too!

Illustration Credits: Associated Press, pp. 5, 10, 24, 27, 35, 41, 43, 59, 67, 76, 83, 84, 93;
Nicole DiMella, p. 50; Everett Digital, pp. 5, 18, 57, 72; Jim Gathany, Centers for Disease
Control/Public Health Image Library, p. 63; Photos.com, pp. 5, 7, 16, 22, 32; Shutterstock,
pp. 3, 5, 14, 20, 30, 46, 52, 55, 79, 87, 89, 91.

Cover Illustrations: Shutterstock (large photo); BananaStock (small inset photo).

C o n t e n t s

Teen Sexual Behavior   1

There once was a time in America when it was considered wrong to have sex before marriage. This was especially true for teenagers. Today, though some people still hold this view, it is not as widespread, and it may be hard for you to imagine. But in the days before the 1960s, most young people abided by the strict rules of the day regarding sexual behavior. You had to follow the rules in order to be considered a moral person.

Young people—especially young women—who disregarded the rules regarding premarital sex risked parental disapproval or punishment. Abortion was illegal in the United States. Young women needing an abortion, with or without their parents' knowledge, would go to Mexico, or even as far as London, to get the procedure. Often the parents of a girl who accidentally became pregnant would send their daughter far away to a home for unwed mothers. There the girl would go through her pregnancy among strangers. Upon giving birth, she would usually be pressured by her family to give the baby up for adoption.

Then, almost overnight, nearly everything about sexual behavior changed.

The Sexual Revolution

In the 1960s, good economic conditions made it easy for young people to put off decisions about marriage and careers. Housing, food, and energy were cheap. A youth counterculture, many of whose members were referred to as "hippies," sprang up to protest limits on personal freedoms. Many marched in huge demonstrations against the Vietnam War, which growing numbers of Americans considered to be an unjust war. This cultural revolution was partly a sexual revolution. Young people felt free to question the traditional values of their parents, lawmakers, and religious leaders, especially those values relating to sexuality.

According to writer Kristin Luker:

> The sexual revolution took place in an atmosphere in which many young people were both critical of established authority and suspicious of the motives of people who wanted to enforce traditional values. Young people were confident their values were authentic and noble ones while their elders were guilty of hypocrisy on a society-wide scale. And a remarkable number of their elders seemed to agree. Both the sexual revolution, and the gender revolution of which it was part, challenged everything that an older generation had taken for granted about men and women, gender and sex.[1]

Free Love

A spirit of "free love," espousing the power of love and the beauty of sex as a natural part of ordinary life, swept the land. Helped along by the introduction of an oral contraceptive known as "the pill," free love became a part of everyday life for many young people. When the birth control pill became widely available in the early 1970s, premarital sex became more common. Birth control information became widely available. By 1973, more liberal attitudes toward abortion led to a major milestone in women's rights—the right to choose. That year the United States Supreme Court, in *Roe v. Wade,* ruled that laws prohibiting abortion violated a woman's right to privacy.

Sexual experimentation became popular, with many young people choosing serial monogamy, a series of relationships with one partner at a time. Some even chose to have multiple sexual partners rather than a monogamous relationship.

As the sexual revolution picked up steam, people learned the hard way that there was a price to pay for "free love"—sexually transmitted diseases (STDs). There was a dramatic increase in cases of gonorrhea, syphilis, and herpes by the late 1960s and throughout the 1970s. So "free love" often wasn't free. By the mid-1980s, people became aware of the spread of a new and deadly STD known as AIDS (acquired immunodeficiency syndrome). Although virtually all STDs except herpes were curable, HIV/AIDS was fatal. For many, the sexual revolution lost its appeal. Later, however, by the late 1990s, the tide turned again with the development of more effective ways of controlling the AIDS infection.

In 2000, journalist Tom Wolfe offered this observation:

> Only yesterday boys and girls spoke of embracing and kissing (necking) as getting to first base. Second base was deep kissing, plus groping and fondling this and that. Third base was oral sex. Home plate was going all the way. That was yesterday. Here in the year 2000 we can forget about necking. Today's boys and girls have never heard of anything that dainty. Today's first base is deep kissing, now known as tonsil hockey, plus groping and fondling this and that. Second base is oral sex. Third base is going all the way. Home plate is learning each other's names.[2]

A couple at the Woodstock rock concert in 1969. The sixties ushered in a new era of sexual freedom.

Sex Makes the World Go Round

Americans are bombarded daily by sexual messages beamed at them by the media. Advertisements for practically every kind of product include images with overt or sometimes suggested sexual connotations. Women and men flaunting idealized bodies, often only partially clothed, cavort across the TV screen. Their job is to get people to spend their money on a particular product or service. They attempt to capture eyeballs by hinting that they are about to engage in lovemaking somewhere off camera.

According to Sabrina Weill, former editor-in-chief of *Seventeen,* founding executive editor of *Cosmo Girl,* and editor of Scholastic's teen health magazine *Choices,* a recent study by the Rand Corporation showed a correlation between teens who watch a lot of sex on TV and teens who have sex at a younger age. And this wasn't talking about R-rated movies. The study found that shows that talk a lot about sex or have a lot of sexual innuendo have just as much of an impact as those that show sex. This came as no major surprise to anyone; obviously TV influences our behavior, or else advertisers wouldn't spend so much money promoting products via commercials.[3]

Because there is so much money to be made, TV is not the only place sex is used to sell something. Magazines are full of sexual images. Advertisements featuring such images also appear on the sides of buses and on giant billboards.

It is hard to avoid exposure to sexual messages. Movies and TV shows, especially on cable TV, often feature partial or even full nudity. The depiction of sexual acts has become almost routine. The music industry also plays a role by churning out sexy music videos as well as songs dripping with explicit lyrics often accompanied by heavy breathing or panting.

In our sex-obsessed culture, it seems that nobody can escape this onslaught from the media. Children often view and hear material they are too young to understand. By the time boys and girls become teenagers, their views about sexuality have often been formed by what they have seen in movies or on TV and the Internet. Pornography, which is easily available on the Internet, often portrays women as sexual objects. Boys whose first erotic experience is looking at hard-core pornography can easily develop a warped view of sex and love. Girls may learn that what is desirable is being servile to men. So it is not surprising that many teens have unrealistic notions about romance and relationships. They may confuse sex with love. And they may not understand the importance of taking responsibility for their actions.

Teen Relationships

As you change from a child to a young adult, your body is developing and your hormones are going wild. You are filled with curiosity about what is happening to you and how you should deal with it. Your first attempts at romantic relationships are likely to be filled with awkward and embarrassing moments. This is especially true when you share your first moments of physical intimacy. You want to appear confident, to show your partner that you know what you are doing, but inwardly you struggle with insecurities. The kind of sexual intercourse you have, especially at first, will be nothing like the idealized kind of sex shown in movies.

It is understandable if you, like many other teenagers, become confused when you attempt to integrate sex into your life. The adults in your life may add to your confusion. Should you or shouldn't you have sexual intercourse? Is it wrong? Why or why not? Why should you wait until you are older or married? You want to do the right thing, but what might seem right for you or your friends might not seem right to your parents.

According to Kristin Luker:

> Many Americans object to the idea of "casual" sex, meaning sex that is not closely linked to the process by which people form couples and settle down. Yet teenagers, especially young teenagers, are almost universally regarded as too young to "get serious" and contemplate marriage. The kinds of sex that *are* appropriate for them (short-term

relationships for the purpose of pleasure, not procreation) run counter to the basic values espoused by many adults. This double bind, according to which serious commitments are premature but casual sex is immoral, makes sexual activity among teens inherently troubling for many adults and ... can make it very difficult for teens to manage their sexual lives.[4]

Teens need to find answers to their questions about sex. Often parents are too embarrassed to discuss sexual questions, even if they know the answers.

"I do think it is hard for us as parents, because we did not have parents who spoke to *us* with relative ease on this subject, if at all," says Karen Hoskins, an Oregon mother of three. "I have just tried to be as honest as I can, and keep any embarrassing thoughts in the back of my mind. I want them to see my honesty and remember it, and then hope they will come to me when they need to ask something."[5]

Some parents may have difficulty because they are unsure of their own values. According to writer Judith Levine:

> Squeamish or ignorant about the facts, parents appear willing to accept the pundits' worst conjectures about their children's sexual motives. It's as if they cannot imagine that their kids seek sex for the same reasons they do: They like or love the person they are having it with. It gives them a sense of beauty, worthiness, happiness, or power. And it feels good.[6]

Some parents fear that having a sexually explicit conversation will encourage their child to have sex with a boyfriend or girlfriend. Not surprisingly, many young people seek answers to their sexual questions elsewhere: from friends, TV shows, movies, magazines, and, especially, the Internet. Some spend time communicating online through teen message boards and teen chat rooms. Much of what they learn from these various sources does not reflect the way real people behave in the real world. However, some organizations and Web sites, such as Planned Parenthood and WebMD, do provide useful information about sexual issues.

Adolescence is normally a time of forming new types of relationships,
a process that can be awkward.

According to Sabrina Weill:

The average American teenager watches over three hours of TV a day and spends more than an hour a day online. No teen will ever say that they saw something on TV or in a movie and then ran out to copy it, though teens will admit that on TV and in the movies (and in a different way, on the Internet) sex is made to look pretty casual and carefree.[7]

Teenagers are accustomed to seeing people have casual sex on TV. Such sex is often portrayed as glamorous, fun, and free of negative consequences. Shows such as *Sex and the City* feature young professionals joking about their one-night stands. So young people come to believe that the sexual behavior portrayed in the media is normal, or even expected. As teenagers who are struggling to behave in a way that is considered "normal," they may be encouraged by the media to have sex before they are ready.

Not surprisingly, many young people seek answers to their sexual questions from friends, TV shows, movies, magazines, and, especially, the Internet.

Media Project Director Robin Smalley says that like it or not, Hollywood serves as a sex education counselor for many young-sters. "Writers will say, 'It's not our responsibility to educate. It's our responsibility to entertain.' And they're right," Smalley says. "They shouldn't be put in the position of being educators—but you know, that's what they are." One survey, conducted in 2000, found that teenagers ages 13–15 ranked entertainment media as the leading source of information about sexuality and sexual health.[8]

Sex and Love: Confusing One for the Other

Many teenagers may be conflicted about whether they should have sex. Maybe they are too young. Some may wonder if they need to fall in love first. Perhaps making love, or having sex, with someone means they love that person. Perhaps not.

Parents want their children to share their values, but many find it difficult to discuss sex and other sensitive topics.

Because people often use the term "make love" to describe intercourse, you might think that you need to have sex to express love. However, sex and love are not the same thing. Two people can have sex without feelings of love for each other. On the other hand, couples in love can express their feelings for each other and be intimate without having sex. If you have intense feelings for another person, you may think you are in love when you are really just infatuated. Whether love or infatuation, the important thing is how you deal with it.

When two people have intense feelings for each other, nothing seems more natural than expressing those feelings through sex. It is very easy to be swept away by your feelings. But the decision to have sex should be a matter for the mind, not the heart. If people decide to have sexual intercourse, they must be aware of the possible consequences. And they must also take responsibility for their decisions and their actions.

Sexual intercourse is the form of sex that is most romanticized in the media. So many people think this is the most intimate sex act they can share with another person. Think back to all the images of sex you've seen on TV or in the movies. In such scenes of romantic kissing, passionate thrusting, and sexy moaning, sex is all about pleasure and excitement. What isn't always shown is that sexual intercourse involves risks.

Many girls worry that they will become pregnant. Guys need to understand how they can cause pregnancies. Girls and guys should be aware of the various birth control options that are available. Many teens are also aware of the danger of STDs. They need to know how to protect themselves by practicing safe sex.

Deciding Whether to Have Sex

How will a person know when he or she is ready to have sex? The fact is that every person is different. What is right for one person may not be right for another. Here are a few of the many important things to consider:

Television shows such as *Sex and the City* reflect an accepting attitude toward casual sex.

Do you know enough about how sex works? To be physically ready for sex, guys and girls need to know their own bodies. Heterosexual teenagers need to learn as much as they can about the opposite sex.

Do you understand the importance of practicing safe sex? Do you know about the various methods of birth control, and are you prepared to use condoms?

Are you comfortable enough with your boyfriend or girlfriend to talk about sex? Do you trust each other enough to discuss your thoughts and feelings and possible fears about sex? When talking about sex, it is important to be able to tell each other what you like and what you want. Before having sex, tell each other what sex means to you.

Are you sure you are not being pressured to have sex? Have you been careful not to pressure your girlfriend or boyfriend into having sex? If a guy thinks he needs to pressure a girl into having sex, he is not ready for sex. Guys who are virgins are often teased by their friends into having sex. They may pressure themselves into having sex in order to prove that they are "manly." But having sex will not make someone a "man." Wanting sex for this reason means the guy is most likely not emotionally mature enough to have sex.

Are you having sex just to build up your self-esteem or to be popular? If so, you are not likely to feel better about yourself. Your self-esteem does not come from doing what others think you should do.

Are you ready for the emotional commitment of a sexual relationship? Having sex will usually change your relationship. Most girls and some guys will expect a deeper emotional commitment. If the two of you want different things from the relationship, one or both of you may end up getting hurt. Yet many teens have replaced traditional dating with "hooking up." Though this phase can mean different things, a recent study defined a hookup as "when a girl and a guy get together for a physical encounter and don't necessarily expect anything further."[9]

Sexting: Sexy Texting

Teenagers have recently discovered that their cell phones can be used for a new form of sexual game known as sexting. Sexting is a special type of texting in which a boy or girl sends a cell phone message that is clearly sexual to another teen. The message can consist just of words, or as is often the case, it can have explicit photos or even videos. Kids as young as twelve have been exchanging nude photos of themselves through their cell phones.

Texting is a good way to stay in touch with friends, but teens need to use good judgment.

Teens may think that sexting is fun. But unfortunately, sexting is a dangerous game. Here is what often happens. A girl sends a nude photo of herself to her boyfriend's cell phone. If or when the two teens break up, the boy may send the photo to his friends. Before long the girl's photo may end up on the Internet, where it can be viewed by pedophiles who prey sexually on young people. In addition, inappropriate images can ruin someone's future if they are viewed by college admissions personnel and potential employers.

Sexting is also dangerous in another way: Some teens have actually been arrested for sexting. According to legal experts, taking nude photos of anyone younger than eighteen could be considered the manufacture of child pornography. Sending the nude photo to someone could be considered distribution of child pornography. And receiving and keeping the photo could be considered possession of child pornography. Indeed, a teen convicted of child pornography can face up to ten years in prison and forever be listed as a sex offender. Even parents can face charges if they know their child is sending nude photos. So to be safe rather than sorry, leave out the sex when texting.

According to Karen Heller of the *Philadelphia Inquirer:*

The latest lie teenagers tell themselves is about having "friends with benefits," the ability to have sex, to "hook up," without the attendant drudgery of relationships. This means that kids expose private parts, exchange bodily fluids, risk pregnancy and STDs, but don't have to plan Saturday dates.[10]

How to Say "No" to Sex

Sex should always be consensual—both people must agree about wanting to have sex. Most of us have grown up hearing various kinds of "advice" about how to behave when it comes to sex. These suggestions, while usually false, unfortunately lead to confused notions about sex and cause many young people to act in inappropriate ways. Sexual "guidelines" such as the following are all too common:

"Remember, boys only want one thing from girls."
"If a girl lets you touch her, she's not 'nice.'"
"When they say 'no' they really mean 'yes.'"
"You'd better do it, or he'll leave you for another girl."

There are a number of reasons why people agree to have sex when they really should refuse. If your boyfriend or girlfriend threatens to break up with you unless you have sex, this is probably a good time to say "no." Having sex because your friends are having sex is not a good reason, nor is having sex in order to be popular. Having sex because you want to feel loved is not likely to accomplish this. It is never a good idea to have sex with one person in order to get even with someone else.

Often guys misinterpret some common types of behavior by girls. A guy needs to understand that when a girl wears tight or revealing clothes, this does not imply that she wants to have sex with him. He should also realize that dancing in a sensuous way does not necessarily indicate a desire for sex. If a girl touches her date's arm casually or puts her hand on his chest while talking to him, he should not assume that she wants to have sex. Romantic

It is important for couples to communicate clearly about their expectations and boundaries regarding sex.

kissing and caressing do not automatically signal that a girl is ready to go all the way with her date. Pushing the guy's hands away when she wants him to stop should not give him the idea that she really wants to continue and is just playing hard to get.

If sex is not consensual, it becomes rape. If you hear someone say "no," you need to stop immediately, even if you are in the middle of a heated make-out session. If your partner changes his or her mind, you need to respect that. Unfortunately, date rape is all too common. Many guys do not seem to understand that "no" means "no," and that "no" will not change to "yes" if they try a little harder. "No" means "stop," and if you do not stop, it can be considered date rape. Just because you may have taken someone out to dinner or a movie does not entitle you to a thank you in the form of sex. Nobody has a right to be sexual with another person against their will, including couples who are dating or even married. Just because someone said "yes" once doesn't mean they are always interested.

If you find yourself in a situation where you need to say "no," be sure to speak up loud and clear. Say "NO" or "STOP," and match your actions with your words. If things are getting out of control, do not keep kissing or touching. Stand up when you say "no." Excuse yourself to go to the bathroom. If necessary, ask to be taken home, or call someone to come and get you. A cell phone will come in handy in such a situation.

Homosexuality

As if learning to deal with sexuality were not difficult enough, issues of sexual orientation can cause even more confusion for some teens. Most people seem to be heterosexual, attracted to members of the opposite sex. So does that mean there is something wrong with us if we feel attracted to members of the same sex, or if we are attracted to both men and women?

Until recent times society disapproved of homosexuality. Gays (homosexual men) and lesbians (homosexual women) usually hid their sexuality. They remained "in the closet," living their lives as if they were straight.

According to Beverly, who was interviewed by author Eric Marcus,

> living in the closet was "exhausting and frightening. I never knew when the ax would fall, when someone would turn me in. At any moment, I knew my career could be over. So I watched everything I said, everything I did, to make sure no one would guess the truth. I tell you, it was the hardest thing I ever did in my life. I thought I was going to lose my mind."[11]

Fortunately, today we have come a long way toward acceptance of same-sex attraction and relationships. Movies and TV shows with popular gay or lesbian characters have become more common. The hit movie *Brokeback Mountain* featured two cowboy heroes in a a homosexual relationship. Will, one of the main

Until recently, society generally disapproved of homosexuality, and gay people kept their feelings and behavior secret. Now attitudes are different, as shown in this demonstration in Utah.

characters of the popular TV show *Will and Grace,* is gay, as is his friend Jack. The main character of the cable TV show *South of Nowhere* is a teenage lesbian. It has become much more common for today's gay teens to accept and be open about their own sexuality. Indeed, in some high schools, it is actually considered "cool" to be

Today we have come a long way toward acceptance of same-sex attraction and relationships.

gay or bisexual. Bisexual means being attracted to both sexes—but usually bisexual people choose one partner to be involved with and engage in serial monagamy.

Why are some of us gay and not straight? Do we at some point choose to be gay? According to writer Eric Marcus:

> No one becomes a homosexual any more than a man or woman becomes a heterosexual. Feelings of attraction for one gender or the other are something we become aware of as we grow up. Where exactly these feelings come from and why some of us have strong heterosexual feelings while others have strong homosexual feelings has plenty to do with genetics and biology and nothing to do with sin or morality, though many religious fundamentalists would have you believe just the opposite.[12]

How do we know if we are gay? Is there a special time in our lives when this becomes apparent? Some people say they knew they were gay from the time they were five or six years old.

Other people don't realize they are gay until they are much older, perhaps even when they are married to a person of the opposite sex. It is during their teen years that many people come out to themselves and others about their sexual orientation. After all, this is the confusing time in our lives when all of us feel puzzled about sex and struggle to find answers to our questions.

Vance Smith, who grew up amid cornfields in Colorado, recalls being made fun of and called "gay" as early as first grade. "I didn't even know what it was," he reports. "I didn't know why I didn't like 'guy-type' stuff like sports or why I was always more comfortable hanging out with girls. And I didn't know why I should be punished for it." By middle school, he says, "I always had a girlfriend, hoping people wouldn't know." But he couldn't make himself feel heterosexual, Smith says. And nobody was fooled, anyway.[13]

Today some gay teens no longer wish to be labeled "gay." They do not want their identity to be solely determined by their sexual orientation. According to writer Ritch C. Savin-Williams, for many young people,

> being labeled as gay or even being gay matters little. They have same-sex desires and attractions but, unlike earlier generations, new gay teens have much less interest in naming these feelings or behaviors as gay.… Rather, teenagers are increasingly redefining, reinterpreting, and renegotiating their sexuality such that possessing a gay, lesbian, or bisexual identity is practically meaningless. Their sexuality is not something that can be easily described, categorized, or understood apart from being part of their life in general.[14]

Some gay and lesbian people like the word "queer," reclaiming a term that has historically been an insult.

Where sexual activity has become an accepted, or even expected, part of teenage behavior, some straight teens are also open to sexual experimentation. According to a report in the February 2006 issue of *New York* magazine, a group of mainstream students in a Manhattan high school were identified as the "bi clique." Looked upon as cool kids, these boys and girls engaged in sex with partners regardless of gender. They defined themselves in terms such as "polysexual, ambisexual, pansexual, pansensual, polyfide, bicurious, bi-queer, metroflexible, heteroflexible, heterosexual with lesbian tendencies—or … 'just sexual.'"[15]

The key to knowing whether we are gay, straight, or bisexual is to pay attention to our feelings of attraction. The challenge is being honest with ourselves about what we are feeling and accepting ourselves for who and what we are. There are no scientific tests or stereotypes that determine our sexuality. You will find out through experiences and feelings.

Boston teens march in the annual Gay/Straight Youth Pride march in 2000. Gay/straight alliance clubs in high schools aim to support the rights of gay youth.

Schools have played an increasingly important role in educating students about homosexuality and fostering attitudes of respect and acceptance. Since the early 1990s, the Gay, Lesbian and Straight Education Network (GLSEN) has worked to change the way schools teach about homosexuality. The organization, which has ninety chapters across the country, explains that its official mission is

> to assure that each member of every school community is valued and respected regardless of sexual orientation.... We believe that such an atmosphere engenders a positive sense of self, which is the basis of educational achievement and personal growth.... We welcome as members any and all individuals, regardless of sexual orientation ... or occupation, who are committed to seeing this philosophy realized in K–12 schools.[16]

Among other activities, GLSEN works directly with high school students through its Student Pride Program, which helps set up and maintain gay/straight alliances (GSAs) and similar student groups. As of 1999, more than five hundred GSAs, from New York to Alaska, were registered with the Student Pride Program.

As you might expect, the liberal goal of GLSEN in teaching students about gays and lesbians has run into opposition from conservative community members. Enraged parents, afraid that GLSEN is "promoting the gay agenda," often confront that organization's members with cries of "How can you teach little children about sick and perverted behavior?"; "God created Adam and Eve, not Adam and Steve!"; "You're trying to recruit our children!" and so forth. These attitudes keep many schools from allowing discussion of homosexuality, much less the formation of gay/straight alliances on school grounds.

Conservative parents fear their children are being harmed, morally and physically, by being taught to tolerate homosexuality. Their protests often arise out of their religious beliefs and their desire to raise their children with what they consider to be good values.

In the face of ongoing opposition, however, the promotion of tolerance regarding the reality of homosexuality continues to make progress.

Birth Control   2

Seventeen-year-old Hector and sixteen-year-old Lisa were about to have sexual intercourse with each other for the first time. As they kissed and touched each other all over, they began removing each other's clothes. The two teens were quickly approaching the point of no return as they got ready to go all the way. Then Lisa noticed that Hector had not put on a condom. When she questioned him, Hector said that he didn't like to use condoms because he didn't enjoy sex as much that way. Lisa was not going to risk getting pregnant. She told Hector that he was going to enjoy things even less when they didn't have sex, because the party was over for now.

Hector and Lisa are fictional characters, but their predicament, though imaginary, can be quite real for many teens in similar situations. Are you ready to use birth control when you and your partner have sex?

Although some guys leave birth control up to the girl, both people in a relationship share that responsibility. You need to know how to get and use condoms or other methods of birth control to prevent unplanned or unwanted pregnancies. When no method of birth control is used, there is an 85 percent chance of becoming pregnant within a year. This means that in any year, out of one hundred women who do not use any type of birth control, eighty-five will become pregnant.[1] Unless you are prepared to use birth control every time you have intercourse, you are not ready for sex.

Condoms

There are various methods of contraception, or birth control. These include condoms, birth control pills, diaphragms, IUDs, rings, implantable contraceptives, and several others. Each has advantages and disadvantages. Do you know which type of birth control is the best one for you?

Condoms work very well to prevent unplanned pregnancies. A condom is a sheath, like a fitted balloon that covers the penis. Condoms are usually made of latex or polyurethane plastic. When used correctly, they are a reliable and effective method of birth control. Although there have been instances of condoms breaking, this rarely happens if the condom is used correctly. So it is important that you know how to use them.

Condoms help prevent pregnancy by keeping the guy's sperm from entering the girl's vagina. The guy should put the condom on his penis when it becomes hard, or erect, before intercourse begins. When the guy ejaculates, or comes, his semen stays inside the condom (mostly at the receptacle at the end). This prevents the sperm from traveling into the girl's uterus and fallopian tubes, so the ovum, or egg, cannot be fertilized. After ejaculating, he should carefully remove the condom and throw it away. A condom should never be used more than once.

Condoms are often a preferred choice of contraception for teens. They are popular because they are relatively inexpensive, they work well, and they are easy to buy, easy to carry around, and easy to use. They help you feel safe from an unplanned pregnancy and most STDs. With typical correct use, condoms are about 83 percent effective. This number grows to 98 percent with perfect use.[2] Lubricated condoms are available. One should be careful before using any other type of external lubricants, as they may not be compatible with some condoms and can reduce their strength.

Another kind of condom is known as the female condom. It is less widely available and more expensive than the male condom, but it is another excellent way to prevent unplanned pregnancies by keeping sperm from entering the vagina. The female condom is a thin, strong polyurethane tube that is placed inside the vagina before intercourse begins. After intercourse, it must be removed and thrown away.

Some people feel that having to stop and put on a condom while making love spoils the romance and spontaneity of the moment. Yet it only takes a few seconds to put on the condom and this stops being a problem once you get used to using condoms. Another common complaint

Condoms are often a preferred choice of contraception for teens.

about condoms is that it makes sex seem less intimate because there is less skin-to-skin contact. This is putting the blame in the wrong place. Intimacy and passion have more to do with how two people kiss and touch each other while having sex. Many guys feel that there is an additional benefit in using the condom during intercourse because it makes their penis slightly less sensitive. This allows them to take longer until they ejaculate.

Condoms can be purchased at drugstores and from vending machines. Women's clinics and your local health clinic often

Used properly, condoms
are good at preventing both
pregnancy and STDs.

provide free condoms. Nobody should be embarrassed to buy condoms. Girls as well as guys can easily buy them. Indeed, almost half of all condoms are sold to females.

A debate has been raging for some time as to whether condoms should be given to teens. Some feel that providing condoms to teenagers is like handing them a license to have sex. Others have a more realistic viewpoint. They believe that many teens are likely to engage in sex with or without condoms, and that it would be especially foolish not to provide their children with protection against unplanned pregnancies and STDs.

According to Kristin Luker, contradictions plague parents who want to protect their children "from the myriad dangers—seen and unseen, life-threatening and emotionally bruising—that sex entails these days."[3] Many parents today do not have a clear idea as to what should be the appropriate age for teens to have sex. They wonder how they can encourage the use of contraception without seeming to push their teenage children into having sex before they are ready. Luker writes:

> Adults disapprove of sexual activity and childbearing among unmarried teenagers, but are generally resigned to the fact that such activity takes place. Many adults prefer the lesser of two evils—contraception as opposed to pregnancy—even to the point of allowing schools to dispense contraceptives. But a substantial minority strive to maintain some degree of control in this area and continue to favor parental-consent laws for teenagers who wish to obtain contraception.[4]

The Birth Control Pill

The most popular method of birth control for teenagers is the oral contraceptive, sometimes called simply "the pill." The pill is very effective in preventing unplanned pregnancies, and it is easy to use. You just have to remember to take one pill per day. (The pill is not effective at preventing pregnancy until after the first full month of use.) With perfect use, the pill is 99.7 percent effective at preventing pregnancy. (Perfect use means following directions exactly: not skipping a day, taking the pill at the same time every day, and so on.) Typical use results in a 91 percent rate of effectiveness.[5] (Typical use means following directions, but not being quite as careful and perhaps skipping a day.)

In most states, a girl does not need her parents' consent in order to get birth control pills. She can get the pills at any health clinic or from her doctor, who will give her a prescription she can fill at her local drugstore. To get a prescription, she will need to get a gynecological or pelvic exam. Planned Parenthood and other health clinics provide birth control services for free or on a sliding-scale fee (that is, you pay what you can afford). The birth control pill is, of course, used solely by women. Every so often, there is word of research into birth control pills for men. So far, no such effective pill has appeared.

Most birth control pills contain two types of synthetic female hormones, progestin and estrogen, and are called "combination pills." The hormones in combination pills prevent ovulation. If there is no ovulation, then no egg can be fertilized by the male's sperm, so pregnancy is not possible. There are various advantages of using combination contraceptive pills. They can make menstrual periods more regular, with less cramping and lighter bleeding. Combination pills can also protect against certain types of cancer such as that of the uterus and ovaries. However, these pills may not be a recommended for women who are genetically susceptible to certain cancers. Some women have side effects from the hormones and cannot take the pill. Side effects may include nausea, breast tenderness, edema (bloating), rash, weight gain or weight loss, spotting (menstrual bleeding between periods), or headaches. If a woman experiences serious side effects, she should talk to her doctor about alternate types of birth control.

The Diaphragm and the Cervical Cap

The diaphragm and cervical cap are two types of birth control devices used by women. A girl can get a prescription for these

A nurse shows some of the birth control methods available at a Planned Parenthood clinic, including the pill and injectable contraceptive.

devices from her doctor or nurse practitioner after she has had a gynecological exam.

The diaphragm is a round, soft rubber dome. The cervical cap, a smaller version of the diaphragm, is made of soft latex or plastic. The devices are inserted into the vagina so that they fit over the cervix. The spermicide (a gel or cream that kills sperm) that must be used with these devices helps block sperm from entering the uterus. If the sperm cannot get into the uterus, the ovum, or egg, cannot be fertilized and the woman will not become pregnant. The spermicide must remain in the vagina for at least six hours after intercourse.

Diaphragms and cervical caps come in different sizes. The doctor or nurse practitioner will fit the device so that it matches the woman's cervix size. Unlike condoms, diaphragms and cervical caps can be used over and over again.

It takes practice to use these devices correctly. When used perfectly, the diaphragm is 94 percent effective and the cervical cap is 91 percent effective. The corresponding figure for typical use is 84 percent for both devices.[6]

The IUD

The intrauterine device, or IUD, is usually only provided to adult women. It is not intended for teens, except for those who have already given birth. The IUD is a small plastic device that is fitted and placed inside the uterus by a doctor or trained healthcare professional. It prevents pregnancy by blocking sperm from reaching the ovum. It also prevents a fertilized egg from attaching itself to the wall of the uterus in case an ovum does become fertilized.

The IUD is very effective at preventing pregnancy—close to 99 percent for both perfect and typical uses.[7] Once inserted, the IUD can remain in place in the uterus for five to ten years. However, there are important disadvantages. IUDs are a relatively expensive means of birth control, and can cost as much as $500. Also, there are some serious potential side effects. These include abdominal cramping, increased chance of pelvic inflammatory disease (PID), spotting between periods, and heavier and longer menstrual periods. When the doctor inserts the IUD, there is the risk of tearing the uterus. Some women using the IUD have developed infections and sterility. So for all of the above reasons, the IUD is not one of the most popular methods of birth control.

Other Types of Birth Control

People can buy spermicides at their local drug store without a doctor's prescription. There are a number of different brands. So if a woman develops an allergic reaction to a particular product, choosing a different one may solve the problem. Used alone, these products are not as effective as condoms, but spermicides and condoms used together are more effective than either method alone. Moreover, condoms protect against STDs, which these products do not do. Spermicides are 82 percent effective with perfect use, 71 percent effective with typical use.[8]

The contraceptive sponge, which is inserted in the vagina, is popular with some women, who find it easier to use than a diaphragm or cervical cap. The sponge is a disposable polyurethane foam disc that contains a spermicide. When used perfectly, the contraceptive sponge is 91 percent effective in preventing pregnancy. With typical use, the sponge is 84 percent effective.[9]

Some women prefer birth control in the form of shots rather than pills. A woman can get a shot of Depo-Provera at her doctor's office. Depo-Provera is an injectable hormone that lasts twelve weeks. It is a convenient method of birth control, more than 99 percent effective with perfect use and 97 percent effective with typical use.[10] Like the birth control pill, Depo-Provera may have unpleasant side effects. One significant side effect from long-term use of Depo-Provera is bone loss over a period of time. One should have adequate calcium intake and do weight-bearing exercises to help reduce this bone loss.

Common Myths About How Not to Get Pregnant

Many teens believe myths about birth control. The following statements are all false. Did you think any of them were true? Being aware of the myths can help teens avoid making some serious mistakes.

- You can't get pregnant if it's your first time.

- You can't get pregnant if you're both virgins.

- You can't get pregnant if you're having your period.

- You can't get pregnant if the guy pulls out before he ejaculates or if he doesn't go all the way in.

- You can't get pregnant if you have sexual intercourse standing up.

- You can't get pregnant if you have sex in a pool or a hot tub.

- You can't get pregnant if you douche with a cola soft drink or vinegar after sex.

- You can't get pregnant if you don't have an orgasm, or if you and your partner don't experience orgasm at the same time.

- You can't get pregnant if you jump up and down after sexual intercourse (to get all the sperm out).

- You can't get pregnant if you push really hard on your belly button after sexual intercourse.

- You can't get pregnant if you take a shower or bath right after sexual intercourse.

- You can't get pregnant if you're on top during sexual intercourse.

- You can't get pregnant if you take aspirin and drink a cola soft drink after sexual intercourse.

- You can't get pregnant if you make yourself sneeze for fifteen minutes after sexual intercourse.[11]

Another type of birth control is the contraceptive implant. The implants, made of six thin, flexible rods or tubes, are placed just under the skin of the woman's upper arm by a doctor. A low dose of a synthetic hormone known as levonorgestrel within the rods is slowly released into the woman's body. The hormone prevents the woman from ovulating and thus from becoming pregnant. A popular brand of implant is called Norplant. Norplant provides up to five years of protection against unplanned pregnancy. The implants can be removed at any time.

The patch, yet another type of contraception, is worn like a Band-Aid on the arm, the stomach, or even the buttocks. The patch usually contains both estrogen and a progestin. Over the course of a month, the woman wears three patches, each one lasting a week. During the fourth week no patch is used. The next month, the routine starts again.

A vaginal ring known as the NuvaRing contains the hormones estrogen and progestogen. The rubber ring rests against the cervix, like a diaphragm or cervical cap. Once inserted in the vagina, the ring is left in place for three weeks and is then removed. One week later, the woman inserts a new ring. The hormones from the ring are absorbed through the vagina.

Emergency Contraception

Lisa agreed to have sexual intercourse with Hector after all, even though he refused to use a condom. At first she was reluctant, fearing she might become pregnant. But Hector was very persistent, repeatedly telling Lisa not to worry. They soon became so involved in the intense physical pleasures of the moment that Lisa lost her motivation to stop. Afterward, Lisa was worried that she might become pregnant.

Was it too late to do anything? Fortunately, Lisa had heard about a method of contraception for emergencies. Some people call it the morning-after pill, although this is not an accurate name, since it does not have to be taken the morning after intercourse, and often two pills are taken at once. While it can be taken up to

120 hours or five days after unprotected sex, it is most effective in preventing pregnancy if it is taken within seventy-two hours or three days of intercourse.

Many people think that emergency contraception causes an abortion. However, the pill prevents a pregnancy from happening and therefore makes an abortion unnecessary. A woman takes emergency contraception after intercourse to make sure she does not become pregnant. The pill works by preventing the woman's body from releasing an egg or by preventing the sperm from reaching the egg. Thus, it is a mistake to confuse the emergency contraceptive pill with the abortion pill.

Young women do not need a parent's consent to get emergency contraception. They can purchase the pills, known by the brand name Plan B, at some drugstores. If they are seventeen or older, they can buy the emergency contraceptive pill without a prescription. However, some people believe that unmarried sex is immoral and are opposed to the sale of the emergency contraceptive pill. Among them are some pharmacists who refuse to sell emergency contraception even if the would-be purchaser has a prescription. So if their local drugstore does not sell the pill, women often have to call around to other drugstores.

A woman can also get the pill at a doctor's office, health clinic, or Planned Parenthood offices.

If you take emergency contraception, you may experience certain unpleasant side effects. These include nausea and vomiting, dizziness, sore breasts, headaches, and irregular vaginal bleeding.

If young women are seventeen or older, they can buy the emergency contraceptive pill without a prescription.

Emergency contraception was developed more than twenty-five years ago. It has been used in all kinds of emergency situations— when a condom breaks or comes off during intercourse or when a girl has been forced to have intercourse against her will. If you are sexually active, it is good to have

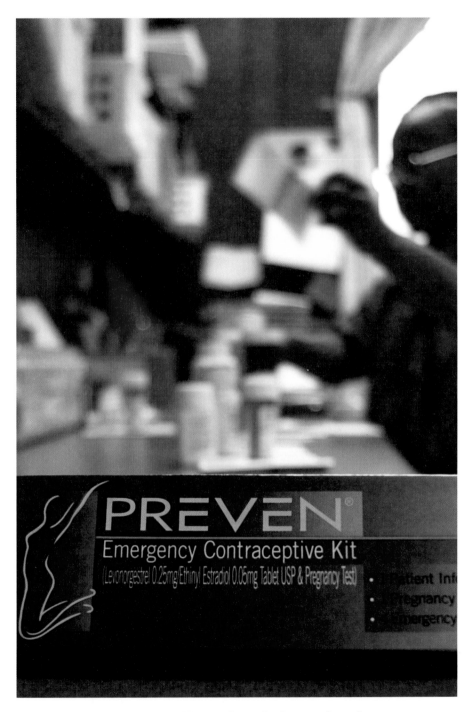

Emergency contraceptive pills, such as the Preven brand, prevent pregnancy with large doses of hormones.

several emergency contraceptive pills handy. You never know when an emergency will occur, and you may not always be able to get the pill when you need it. Remember that emergency contraception should always be used as a backup method, not as regular birth control.

Is Abstinence a Realistic Method of Contraception?

Eighteen-year-old Kayla was a believer in abstinence. All through her teen years, she managed to avoid having sexual intercourse. She had dated several guys. Some of her romantic relationships had lasted for more than a year. There were times when Kayla was strongly tempted to go all the way with her boyfriend. At such times, she would think that, after all, there might not be anything terribly wrong with it. She knew some of her best girlfriends led very active sex lives, but until now, Kayla had held to her beliefs. Then one day, Kayla and her current boyfriend Sean took things to the next level while making love. For the first time, Kayla's feelings and desires grew too powerful to resist. Unfortunately on this occasion, neither she nor her boyfriend had bothered to use condoms or any other type of birth control.

Like Kayla, a fictional character, many people believe abstinence is the best method of contraception. What could possibly be more effective than abstaining from sex? After all, if a woman never has intercourse, she most certainly will not become pregnant. So one could say that abstinence offers 100 percent protection against unwanted pregnancy.

However, is it realistic to rely on abstinence as the only form of contraception for any and all occasions? Indeed, can people trust themselves to never give in to the urge to have sexual intercourse until some time in the future when they are married and planning to start a family? Abstaining from sex takes great discipline, since hormones, feelings, and peer pressure are at a high level during the teen years.

High school and college students march in San Francisco to show their support for abstinence before marriage. Many people believe that abstinence is the only method of birth control that teens need to learn about.

Less-Reliable Contraceptive Methods

The rhythm method, also known as natural birth control, involves using a calendar and body clues, such as temperature and vaginal secretions, to determine when a woman is ovulating. Using the rhythm method effectively takes great discipline—months of training, careful record keeping, and the willingness of both partners to avoid taking risks on "unsafe" days. Many teenagers find this method unreliable, because young women's menstrual cycles are not always regular and because their relationships can make planning ahead difficult.

One particularly unreliable method of birth control is known as withdrawal. The guy pulls his penis out of the girl's vagina before ejaculation. This is a particularly risky way of attempting to prevent pregnancy. A joke about this method asks, "What do you call people who practice withdrawal?" The answer is "parents." Actually, withdrawal can work if it is practiced perfectly. However, a guy may not be able to control when he ejaculates. If the sperm ends up on the girl's inner thigh or anywhere near the vagina, some of it can seep back inside the vagina. Even the pre-ejaculatory fluid may contain some sperm.

Teen Pregnancy

Sixteen-year-old Tina had never been so scared in her life. It was a cold, rainy day in Seattle in 1970. Two days earlier she had discovered that she was pregnant. What on earth was she going to do? She was afraid to tell her parents. She was even afraid to tell her best friend, Louise. When she told her boyfriend, Rob, he told her not to worry. Everything would be OK.

Rob took Tina to a doctor he knew. The doctor gave Tina a phone number to call. When she called, a man instructed Tina to take the early-morning train from Seattle to Vancouver in Canada. There she would be met by people who would take care of her. Tina had done as she was told. Now as the train sped northward, she was filled with fear.

At the station in Vancouver, two men dressed in black met her. She handed them the money Rob had given her. They took Tina to their car, blindfolded her, and drove her away. The rest of the day remains a blur in Tina's memory. Fortunately, Tina survived her abortion, which was performed in strictest secrecy, and she returned home safely.

Although Tina and Rob are fictional characters in an imaginary situation, Tina's experience was not unusual. In the days before *Roe v. Wade,* abortion was illegal in the United States. It was also very dangerous, often being performed by unlicensed doctors or even persons without medical training. In those days, it was fairly typical for girls facing an unwanted pregnancy to go to Canada, Mexico, or even as far away as England for an abortion, or to get one illegally in the United States. If Tina had confided in her parents, they might have insisted that she go through with the pregnancy and then give up the baby for adoption. They probably would have sent her away to a home for unwed mothers.

That was then. Today, teenage girls who become pregnant do not face such harsh choices. Abortion has been legal in the United States since the U.S. Supreme Court's 1973 decision in *Roe v. Wade.* It is also still possible to give birth and give the baby up for adoption. If marriage is not in the cards, being an unwed mother today does not carry quite the social stigma it did in the past. Single moms are not at all unusual. Indeed, in 2006, for the first time in United States history, a majority of all births to women under thirty—50.4 percent—were out of wedlock.[1] Still, an unplanned pregnancy can result in huge hardships for a young woman. It is essential that such a person make the right choice.

Choices for Pregnant Teenagers

If a girl becomes pregnant, she will have to make an important decision that will affect her for the rest of her life: Should she have an abortion, or should she go through the pregnancy and give birth? If she chooses to give birth, she has another decision to make—should she give the baby up for adoption, or should she raise the baby herself? If she decides to raise the child and marriage is not an option, she will become a single mother. These are all very difficult decisions.

Why do so many young women find themselves in such a situation in the first place? And why do so many find it so difficult to make the best decisions for themselves? According to writer Ruth Sidel, professor of sociology at Hunter College:

> Having little understanding about sex, how to prevent pregnancy, what abortion involves, and the process of childbirth is obviously an enormous hindrance to making informed decisions. It is almost inconceivable to many adults that teenagers—despite their classes in sex education in public schools and their massive cultural exposure to sexuality at ever-younger ages through fashion, music, advertisements, videos, movies, and television programming—still lack a genuine understanding of sexuality, human reproduction, how contraception works, and how early childbearing would affect them.[2]

If a girl does not wish to raise a child and is not comfortable with the prospect of having an abortion for whatever reason, she has an alternative option. She can give birth and give up the baby for adoption. This is also a difficult choice: On one hand, she may feel unready to raise a child herself, knowing that it will affect her prospects for education, employment, and social life. On the other hand, she may feel that by relinquishing a child for adoption, she is giving away her own flesh and blood.

There are two kinds of adoption: closed adoption and open adoption. In a closed adoption, the names of the birth mother and the adoptive parents are kept secret from one another. In an open adoption, the names of the birth mother and the adoptive parents are known to one another. Both kinds of adoption are legal and binding.

There are various ways of doing an adoption. An adoption agency will present the baby to a couple or family who may be better prepared to raise a child to adulthood. In an agency adoption, the birth parents relinquish their child to the agency. The agency then places the child into the adoptive home. Most adoptions conducted by agencies are closed adoptions.

The agency adoption is a licensed adoption. In an independent or unlicensed adoption, the birth parents relinquish their child directly into the adoptive home. An independent adoption can be arranged through a doctor or lawyer or someone else who knows a couple that wants to adopt. In yet another type of adoption, the court grants legal adoption to relatives.

Is Abortion a Beneficial or Harmful Alternative?

For many pregnant teens, abortion may be the best choice. Advocates of abortion rights, those who are "pro-choice," argue that a woman has the right to control what happens to her own body. While not recommending that women have abortions, pro-choice advocates support the pregnant woman's right to have that as an option. Many people especially support the right to abortion in cases of rape or incest or when the mother is too young to care for the child. Early motherhood can result in many lost opportunities for the girl. Teen mothers are less likely to complete

If a girl becomes pregnant, she will have to make an important decision: Should she have an abortion, or should she go through the pregnancy and give birth?

their education[3] and more likely to have limited careers.[4] They are also more likely to be poor.[5] Supporters of a woman's right to choose also argue that bringing a child into the world before a girl is ready is also unfair to the child.

Meanwhile, opponents of choice believe that the fetus is a human being with a fundamental right to life. They conclude that abortion is murder and immoral. Some people argue that having an abortion can result in low self-esteem, feelings of guilt, difficulty with relationships, substance abuse, and other problems.

If a woman is considering an abortion, she should contact Planned Parenthood or the National Abortion Federation. These

Deciding What to Do

If a girl is pregnant and is trying to decide whether to have an abortion, coming up with answers to the following questions will help her make the decision:

- Am I ready (financially, emotionally, mentally) to raise a person from birth to adulthood?

- What kind of support would I get from the baby's father?

- What kind of support would I get from my family and from the father's family?

- How would I feel if I put the baby up for adoption?

- How would I feel if I had an abortion?

- Can I afford to have an abortion?

- Would I prefer to have a child at another time?

- What would it mean for my future and my family's future if I had a child now?

- Do I have strong religious beliefs about abortion?

- How do I feel about other women who have abortions?

- How important is it to me what other people will think about my decision?

- Can I handle the experience of having an abortion?

- Is anyone pressuring me to have an abortion? Am I being pressured not to have an abortion?

- Would I be willing to tell a parent or go before a judge if my state requires it?

A march for abortion rights in Washington, D.C. Pro-choice advocates believe that women should have the right to choose abortion.

organizations will help her with making her decision. They will also help locate a doctor who is able to perform the abortion safely. Not all Planned Parenthood clinics perform abortions. Women in rural areas may have to travel across the state (or into another state) to find a doctor who does.

Some states now have laws that require parental permission for a female under age eighteen to have an abortion. Planned Parenthood or the National Abortion Federation can tell you what your state laws are.

Today, a legal abortion performed by a qualified doctor is safe. The most widely used method of abortion is called vacuum aspiration. This procedure can be performed up to sixteen weeks of pregnancy. Another type of procedure is a D&E (dilatation and evacuation). This is usually performed between the sixteenth and twenty-fourth weeks of pregnancy. Another type of abortion uses medication to end the pregnancy. An abortion pill called mifepristone (formerly called RU 486) is usually used. Sometimes, a pill known as methotrexate is used instead. Medication abortions can be performed up to sixty-three days (nine weeks) after the woman's last period.

Factors Contributing to Teen Pregnancy

A long list of factors, many related to each other, contribute to America's high rate of teen pregnancies. These include poverty, lack of parental guidance, sexual abuse, lack of services for teens, use of drugs and alcohol, lack of information, and a general ignorance about sexuality and contraception.

Growing up in poverty or in a dysfunctional family can often limit hopes teenagers may have for the future. They can look forward to more poverty, limited job opportunities, and difficult lives in general. Teens who do not have a close and open relationship with their parents are more likely to become pregnant than those who do.

Many such girls come to regard motherhood as the only role available to them. Having a child is seen as an act of hope, a chance for a better life, at least for the child.

Some teens engage in risky sexual behavior, believing that they will never suffer unwanted consequences. They feel that they can have sex without protection and never become pregnant. In the words of one professional who works with teen mothers, "Ninety percent thought it would never happen to them. They never, ever thought they would get pregnant."[6]

Risky behavior is not all that unusual for Americans, and a propensity for taking risks seems to be ingrained in the American psyche. According to writer Lynn Ponton, a clinical psychiatrist and professor of psychology at the University of California at San Francisco:

Many young couples faced with an unplanned pregnancy did not think it could ever happen to them.

> The United States excels in one area ... that of dangerous sexual risk-taking—i.e., unprotected sexual intercourse resulting in unwanted pregnancy and sexually transmitted diseases. For generations, this country has struggled with adolescent risk-taking of all types. American culture is defined by risk-taking—the successful pursuit of the American Dream virtually requires it—but we are not a society particularly adept at risk assessment.[7]

Among those teens more likely to engage in high-risk sexual behavior are girls who have been sexually abused or exploited by older men and those who drink or use illegal drugs. They are more likely to have sex at a young age, have sex with a greater number of partners, and neglect to use birth control than are girls who have not been sexually abused and do not drink or use drugs.

While many young women don't seem to realize that sexual intercourse without contraception is likely to lead to pregnancy, others do understand but are still reluctant to use birth control. In a throwback to the 1950s, some people still cling to the idea that it is OK for guys to be sexually active (and such young men are approvingly called "studs" or "real men"), but that only "bad girls" plan for sex. Because of this, many girls seem to fear that by using contraception and protecting themselves against pregnancy, they will earn the label of "slut."[8] Girls should understand that being prepared for sex doesn't make them pushy or easy—it just makes them smart.

Teen Birth Rates: Troubling Statistics

On December 5, 2007, the National Center for Health Statistics released a disturbing report. For the first time in fourteen years, there was an increase in teen birth rates. There was debate among experts as to the nature and cause of the 3 percent increase.[9] Was it just a temporary upward blip in a long-term downward trend, or was it the start of a climb toward ever-higher rates of teen pregnancies and births?

Before this latest report, health experts were optimistic that a combination of educational campaigns and the HIV/AIDS epidemic would continue to reduce the numbers of teens becoming pregnant. Fewer teens were having sexual intercourse, and condom use was increasing. Some people, mainly religious conservatives, believed that abstinence-only educational programs were having a beneficial effect. After all, the 34 percent decline in the teen birth rate from 1991 to 2005 seemed reason enough for the optimism. The teen birth rate was twenty-one per one thousand young women aged fifteen to seventeen in 2005, an all-time low. That was down from thirty-nine births per one thousand teens in 1991.[10]

Also in 2005, 47 percent of high schoolers—6.7 million— reported having had sexual intercourse, down from 54 percent in 1991. Of those who had sex during a three-month period in 2005,

63 percent—about 9 million—used condoms, up from 46 percent in 1991.[11] Hopefully, these statistics will continue to improve, but only time will tell. Meanwhile, America still has very high numbers of teens who give birth each year. Eleven percent of all births in the United States each year are to teens. About 750,000 pregnancies in the United States occur among girls aged fifteen to nineteen.[12] This is higher than in any other industrialized nation. Eight in ten of teen pregnancies are unintended.[13]

Should Society Approve of Teen Parenting?

As society has become more accepting of premarital sex in recent years, so has it come to regard teen parenting as more or less acceptable. As with other aspects of sexuality in America, society's response to teen parenting has generated heated debate. Some believe that society should help teen mothers as much as possible and provide for their basic needs. They support programs such as Florence Crittenton Homes, which offer young mothers a supportive place to live while they raise their babies. Others believe that society's acceptance of teen motherhood only encourages more teens to have babies.

Today, the large numbers of unwed mothers, including celebrity mothers such as Jamie Lynne Spears, have helped to greatly reduce the social stigma that once caused pregnant teens to have their babies in secret. In many places today, pregnant teens can live fairly normal lives. In some high schools, they can become cheerleaders or members of the student council. Some high schools even provide day care for student mothers.

Such support does not exist everywhere. In 1999, U.S. District Judge William Bertelsman ruled that two Kentucky teenagers who had gotten pregnant could not be excluded from the National Honor Society.[14] Yet many people strongly believe that the National Honor Society should most definitely not accept students who have gotten pregnant. They argue that the National Honor Society was correct to deny admission to the two teen mothers.

While births among U.S. teens have decreased in recent years, the pregnancy rate is still higher than in any other industrialized nation.

According to them, the Honor Society should require a higher moral standard from students they accept. Unwed mothers, even if they do well in school, are not good role models, they say.[15]

Some people believe that not only should society not accept teen pregnancy, but that it should strongly condemn teenage sexuality and childbearing. According to these folks, the main cause of teenage pregnancy in the United States is the sexually permissive attitudes of today's teens. The debate in America over the causes and solutions to the problem of teen pregnancy and childbearing is destined to continue.

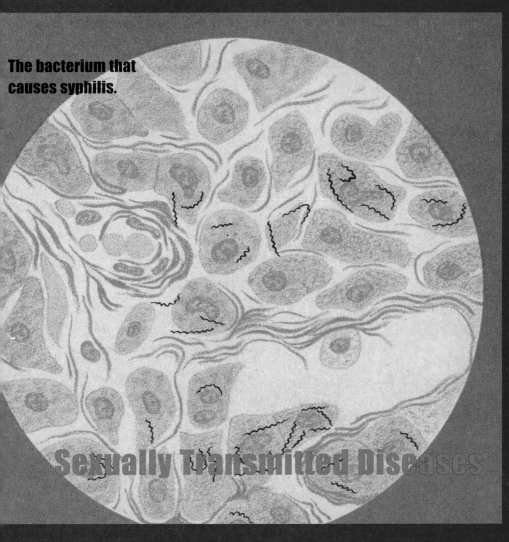

The bacterium that causes syphilis.

Tony had had sexual intercourse with many partners by the time he was seventeen. In the back of his mind, Tony was aware that STDs (sexually transmitted diseases) existed, but he had never been particularly careful about protecting himself. Like many teenagers, Tony believed that STDs would not happen to him. Also, Tony, like many other guys, believed that using a condom reduced the degree of pleasure in sex. A few of his partners had insisted that he use condoms and had provided them for him. Most of the time, Tony went without, exposing himself and his partner to the danger of STDs.

One morning when Tony went to the bathroom to urinate, he felt a painful, burning sensation in his penis. He knew something was *wrong. His symptoms persisted, so Tony went to the doctor. He learned that he was suffering from an STD—gonorrhea. Tony's luck had run out. For a long time he had been engaging in risky sexual behavior. Now he was paying for it.*

Sex: Safer, Safe, Unsafe

Tony is a fictional character in an imaginary situation. However, people in the real world often find themselves in a similar predicament. Are you ready to practice safer sex? Although some guys, like Tony, leave protective measures up to the girl, both people in a relationship share that responsibility. Until you know how to get and use condoms to protect against STDs, you are not ready to have sex.

Many teens today have misconceptions about STDs and how they are spread. According to a Kaiser Family Foundation survey in 2003:

- Twenty-five percent of fifteen- to seventeen-year-olds said that they would know if someone they were dating had an STD.

- Twenty percent thought that STDs can only be spread when symptoms are present.

- Twelve percent believed that "unless you have had sex with a lot of people, STDs are not something you have to worry about."

- Ten percent agreed with the statement: "STDs are a nuisance, but they do not have any serious health effects."[1]

STDs have been spreading through the teenage population at an alarming rate. A federal study in March 2008 reported:

One in four American girls between the ages of 14 and 19—and nearly half of all African-American girls in that same age range—are infected with at least one of four sexually transmitted diseases: human papillomavirus (HPV), chlamydia, genital herpes, and trichomoniasis.[2]

Marchers in Philadelphia demonstrate in favor of providing information about condoms to teens in 2004. Condoms are important in preventing the spread of STDs.

There are many kinds of STDs, all of which are caused either by viruses, bacteria, or parasites. It is very easy to get an STD, and people need to protect themselves. Unsafe sex is sex without the use of a condom. This applies to giving or receiving vaginal sex, oral sex, and anal sex. It applies to same-sex activity as well as heterosexual activity. Obviously, if you want to avoid STDs, you should not practice unsafe sex. In the words of one HIV-prevention poster, "No glove, no love."

In addition, keep in mind that people can express physical intimacy in other ways. Hugging is perfectly safe. The risk of catching an STD from kissing is fairly remote.

Safer sex practices, while never 100 percent safe, are still reasonably effective in preventing the spread of STDs. Latex and plastic condoms offer protection against most STDs. However, they may not offer complete protection against such viruses as HPV (which causes genital warts), because areas infected with the virus may be outside the areas covered by the condom. Condoms must be used each time you have sex. They must be used correctly. If you wait until you are ready to ejaculate to put on the condom, you are not practicing safer sex.

Having monogamous sexual relationships greatly reduces your chances of contracting an STD. Monogamy means having sex with only one partner, who only has sex with you. But monogamy is no guarantee against becoming infected with an STD. Your partner may have been at risk for STDs in the past. He or she may be infected and not know it. Since it is possible to have an STD and not show any symptoms, you and your partner should get tested to see if either of you is infected with an STD. Some teenagers mistakenly believe that serial monogamy will protect them from STDs. They think that by having sex with only one person at a time, even if each relationship lasts only a few weeks, they do not need to use a condom. Such behavior can only be classified as unsafe sex.

Getting Tested for STD Infections

Regular checkups for STDs are an important part of maintaining sexual health for teens as well as for adults. Testing for sexually transmitted infections will allow both you and your partner to know if one of you is infected with STDs and to deal with it before you become intimate.

Certain doctors who do not specialize in STDs may not have access to the most up-to-date information about them. It is impor-tant that you find someone who has the necessary expertise and with whom you feel comfortable talking. You must be able to trust this doc-tor to provide supportive, nonjudg-mental sexual health care and coun-seling. Your health care provider is bound by the rules of practice to

Having monogamous relationships—having sex with only one partner, who only has sex with you—greatly reduces your chances of contracting an STD.

protect your privacy. All teenagers in the United States have the right to diagnosis and treatment of STDs without the consent or knowledge of their parents or guardian.

Testing can be done confidentially, meaning your records are not released to anyone without your written permission. In some instances, testing can be done anonymously, meaning you do not use your full name when you are tested. Because you use only your first name or some other name, there is complete anonymity. Only you know that you are being tested and what the results of the testing are.

If you are diagnosed with gonorrhea, syphilis, AIDS, or chlamydia, this fact must be reported to the state or local health department. The laws governing the reporting of STDs vary from state to state. In general, the health departments will help those who have been diagnosed with STDs in anonymously contacting partners to be tested and treated. The name of the person with the infection is not revealed. This information is not released to any other individuals or organizations, such as insurance companies.

In the future, health clinics across America may offer routine HIV testing to everyone who seeks medical care, no matter the symptom. Two years ago, federal health officials recommended routine HIV testing for all Americans aged thirteen to sixty-four. Although some doctors agreed with the recommendation, others believed that such extensive testing was not necessary. So such a program was not established. Now, however, some communities are taking another look at the issue. In June 2008, New York City announced a new program to offer HIV tests to nearly every patient in the city. The program will first focus on residents of the Bronx, one of the five boroughs of New York City. The Bronx has been especially hard hit by the AIDS epidemic. In 2006, 357 Bronx residents died from AIDS, about a third of all AIDS deaths in the city.[3]

Chlamydia: The Most Common Bacterial STD

Chlamydia is the most common sexually transmitted bacterial disease in the industrialized world. At least 4 to 6 million people are infected with chlamydia each year in the United States. Among women, symptoms include a frequent need to urinate, burning with urination, a discharge from the genital area, pelvic pain, and bleeding between periods or after intercourse. Symptoms for guys include burning with urination, a clear or yellowish discharge from the penis, an itchy or irritated feeling in the urethra, and redness at the tip of the penis. Symptoms usually disappear about three weeks after exposure.

Upon diagnosis, doctors prescribe antibiotics. When treated, chlamydia causes no lifelong problems. Left untreated, it can damage a woman's reproductive system and cause infertility, the inability to have children. Complications in men can include infection of the prostate gland, the urethra, and the epididymis. This can result in scarring and infertility.

Many women and men infected with chlamydia have no symptoms. They are usually surprised when they test positive. A person

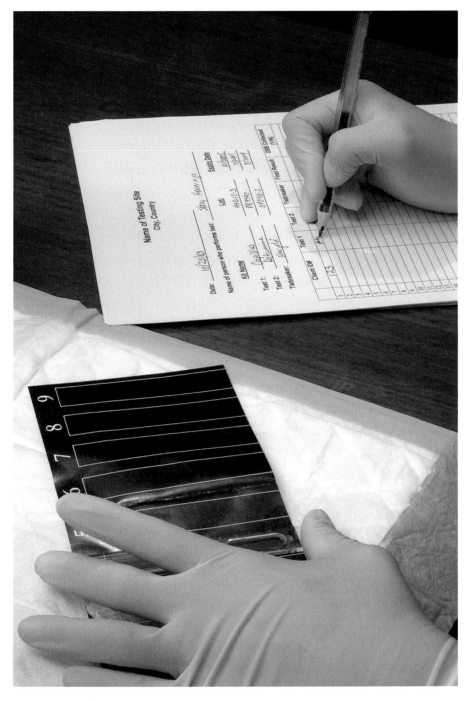

A technician records information on an AIDS test. Confidential STD screening and treatment is available to all teens in the United States.

can be free of symptoms for weeks, months, or years after becoming infected. Some people remain symptom-free for life. Because many people who have chlamydia experience no symptoms, they are unaware that they have the disease, and they often unknowingly pass the disease to their partners. Therefore, it is important that sexually active teens get tested regularly for chlamydia.

Genital Herpes: The STD That Never Goes Away

Genital herpes is a common viral STD; it is so common that about one of four adults in America is infected with it. Unfortunately, once you get it, you can never get rid of it. The virus stays in your system throughout your life. Herpes has been around for a very long time. The ancient Egyptians described its symptoms in their medical texts. The word "herpes," which comes from the ancient Greeks, means "to creep." The name suggests the way herpes sores can spread to different parts of the body.

There are two types of herpes, which are caused by the herpes simplex virus (HSV). Type I herpes, oral herpes, results in sores on the mouth, also known as fever blisters or cold sores. According to Lisa Marr, MD:

> Approximately 70 percent of adults have oral herpes by the time they reach the age of forty, although there is some thought that HSV-1 infection—the usual cause of oral herpes—is becoming less common in childhood now than in the past. Most people acquire oral herpes through nonsexual transmission before the age of five, such as from an adult with oral HSV-1 who kisses them or from other children.[4]

Type II herpes, genital herpes, can cause painful blisters, sores, or red-rimmed bumps on the penis, vulva, anus, and even on the mouth. Itching and burning are common symptoms. You can experience outbreaks of herpes one or two times a year, especially if you are physically run down or under stress. Some people, however, never get another outbreak after the first time. There are also those who never experience any symptoms and are unaware they have the infection.

Unfortunately, herpes is very contagious. You can get it just by kissing someone who is infected, or by any oral contact or oral sex. In recent years, it is getting harder and harder to tell whether someone has Type I or Type II herpes. A person who has cold sores on his or her mouth may actually have genital or Type II herpes on the mouth. The two types of herpes are increasingly becoming intermixed. The only good news is that whenever you experience an outbreak, there is medication you can take to get rid of the symptoms. Scientists are currently testing vaccines that it is hoped will prevent symptoms in those infected with the herpes virus.

Human Papillomavirus: Genital Warts

Human papillomavirus (HPV) has become the most common STD in the United States. There are more than a hundred types of human papillomavirus. Most people have at least one type. It is estimated that 75–80 percent of sexually active adults have or have had HPV. With most people, the human papillomavirus, like the herpes virus, never goes away once you become infected. Not everyone infected by HPV develops genital warts. For those who do, the warts can recur throughout life. However, researchers believe that in some people, the virus eventually disappears.

The genital warts are small, painless flesh-colored bumps that can be itchy in some cases. They can form and grow on a guy's or girl's genitals, including the penis, the pelvic area, the anus, the vulva, and inside the vagina. Genital warts are very contagious and are spread through skin-to-skin contact. Doctors remove the warts either by burning them off or freezing them with liquid nitrogen.

For some people, HPV can be a very dangerous virus. Each year in the United States, hundreds of thousands of women and girls develop infections from it. Among this group, more than ten thousand develop cervical cancer and thirty-seven hundred die from the cancer. For forty years, doctors have relied on the Pap smear test to screen women for cervical cancer. The test is named after George Papanicolaou, the man who developed it.

Detection of cancer or precancerous changes makes it possible to begin treatment that can either cure or prevent cervical cancer.

According to Lisa Marr, "The Pap smear is recommended as a screen for all women over the age of eighteen, or earlier if a woman becomes sexually active at a younger age. *All* women, not just young women, need to be screened for cervical cancer."[5]

Gardasil, the HPV Vaccine

There is now a vaccine called Gardasil that can protect girls against four types of HPV—HPV 6, 11, 16, and 18. HPV 16 and 18 are responsible for causing more than 70 percent of cervical cancers.[6] And HPV 6 and 11 cause about 90 percent of genital warts cases. The Gardasil vaccination consists of a series of three shots. Gardasil proved very effective at preventing infection from HPV 16 and 18. And according to Jesse L. Goodman, director of the FDA's Center for Biologics Evaluation and Research, "There is now strong evidence that this vaccine can help prevent vulvar and vaginal cancers due to the same viruses for which it also helps protect against cervical cancer."[7]

The Food and Drug Administration approved Gardasil on June 8, 2006. Because this vaccine had proven to be so effective, less than a month later federal health officials at the Centers for Disease Control proposed that a Gardasil vaccination should be given to all females between the ages of nine and twenty-six. Their reasoning was based on data indicating that the vaccine works best before girls become sexually active. For these girls, the vaccine can prevent almost 100 percent of disease caused by the four types of HPV targeted by the vaccine.[8] Many states, including California and Texas, suggested making the vaccination mandatory for all middle school girls.

These suggestions have provoked heated debate within the medical community. Some doctors are concerned that long-term side effects of the vaccine are unknown at this point. According to Dr. Karen McCune, an associate professor of obstetrics and

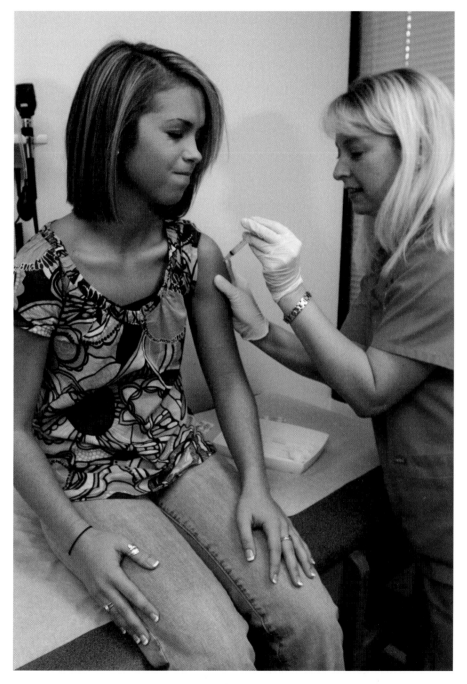

A young woman receives a shot of Gardasil, the HPV vaccine. HPV is responsible for more than 70 percent of cervical cancers, so the vaccine offers important protection to women.

gynecology at UCSF, "At this stage, vaccination can still be considered experimental. To be discussing mandatory vaccination when the main clinical trials are still ongoing seems extremely premature. We're feeling like the enthusiasm is driving policy rather than data."[9] Dr. Neal Halsey, a professor in the department of International Health and Pediatrics at the Johns Hopkins Bloomberg School of Public Health, director of the Institute of Vaccine Safety, and chair of the vaccine group at the Infectious Diseases Society of America, says, "We're pushing too early, too fast.... It is a very valuable, very useful vaccine—our first for cancer—so let's do it right."[10] (Note that Gardasil is not literally a cancer vaccine, but a vaccine against a virus that can cause cancer.)

Other opposition to mandatory vaccination has come from Christian conservatives and advocates of an abstinence-only approach to sex. They argue that making sex safer only encourages young people to become more sexually active. The growing antivaccine movement also includes parental-rights supporters, who resent any mandates regarding how parents handle their children's health. Then there are the consumer rights activists who suspect the motives of giant pharmaceutical companies that have a track record of putting profits before safety.

Deborah Arrindell, vice president of health policy at the American Social Health Association, believes that when parents become educated about Gardasil, they are likely to approve of the vaccination for their children. According to journalist Karen Houppert, Arrindell believes:

It is vital to mandate the shots. That's because leaving the shots voluntary means some girls will get them, but a lot won't. And those who won't get the shots are those who can't afford them. Mandating the vaccine makes it much more likely that insurers will cover the costs, that Medicaid will pay and that federally funded vaccine programs will quickly offer free vaccines for uninsured children.[11]

Summing up her estimation of the benefits of the Gardasil HPV vaccine, Arrindell says, "This is the best public health news we've had for women in fifty years. It's huge. It's exciting. It's wonderful.... It's a good thing."[12]

Trichomoniasis

Trichomoniasis, often called "trich," is one of the most common STDs. It is caused by a tiny single-celled parasitic protozoan organism known as *Trichomonas vaginalis*. The tiny parasite is found in the vagina or urethra. Trich is almost always spread by vaginal sex. Using condoms correctly helps prevent transmission of the disease.

Each year, about 3 million women in the United States are diagnosed with trich. There are no statistics for the number of men infected, because most men with this STD do not develop any symptoms. In women, typical symptoms include a yellow-green discharge from the vagina; vaginal itching, irritation, and redness; and a fishy odor from the vagina. Some women may also experience burning with urination and pain in the abdomen. A few men infected with trichomoniasis experience symptoms of urethritis: burning with urination, discharge, or a sensation of irritation in the penis. If left untreated, trich in men can cause scarring in the urethra, which may impair the flow of urine.

About half the women infected with trich have no symptoms. However, they are carriers and can pass the infection along to others. Men can be carriers and pass it along as well, without even knowing they have it. When detected, trichomoniasis can be easily treated with antibiotics. Oral antibiotics are about 95 percent effective in treating trichomoniasis. Condoms, if used correctly, help prevent the transmission of trichomoniasis.

Gonorrhea: The Oldest STD

Gonorrhea has been around since the beginning of history. The word "gonorrhea," which comes from the ancient Greeks, means "flow of seed." During the fourteenth century, gonorrhea acquired its common nickname, the "clap." Gonorrhea is caused by the gonorrhea bacterium known as *Neisseria gonorrhoeae.* It is named after Albert Neisser, a German doctor who first identified the germ in 1879. He also proved that gonorrhea was a separate disease from syphilis, which some doctors had believed to be a new form of gonorrhea.

More than six hundred thousand people are infected with gonorrhea each year in the United States. Although this overall number has been decreasing, the number of sexually active young people infected with the disease has been increasing. Women aged fifteen to nineteen have the highest reported rates of gonorrhea. Gonorrhea is very easy to transmit through sexual contact. A girl having unprotected sex with an infected guy has an 60 to 90 percent chance of catching it each time they have intercourse. For a guy, the risk of catching gonorrhea from an infected girl is 20 to 50 percent each time.[13] The infection is spread through vaginal, oral, or anal sex. The best protection against the disease is using a condom. Some girls who use birth control pills do not use condoms when having intercourse. They mistakenly believe that the pill will protect them from STDs.

The most common symptom of gonorrhea in men is a discharge, usually yellow, from the penis. This is accompanied by a burning sensation with urination or just an irritated feeling in the penis. The most common symptom of gonorrhea in women is a yellow discharge from the vagina and spotting between periods or after sexual intercourse. One in five women who have untreated gonorrhea will develop pelvic inflammatory disease (PID).[14] PID is an infection of a woman's reproductive system, affecting the uterus and fallopian tubes. It can be a very painful condition. Although most people with gonorrhea have symptoms, some men and women who get the infection do not have any symptoms and do not know they are carrying the infection.

If untreated, gonorrhea can cause scarring in the genital area, which can lead to fertility problems in both women and men.

Gonorrhea can also infect the eyes, joints, heart valves, and lining of the brain and spinal cord, and it can cause sores on the skin. A mother infected with gonorrhea can pass the infection to her baby. The gonorrhea bacteria can infect a baby's eyes shortly after birth, leaving the baby blinded for life. To prevent this, all states require that health care workers administer antibiotic eyedrops every time a baby is born.

Fortunately, gonorrhea can be successfully treated with antibiotics. Some treatments are given as an injection, some as a single pill, and some as a week-long course of oral medication.

Sexual partners of a person with gonorrhea must be treated for the infection as well. This means everyone who has had sexual contact with the infected person in the last sixty days.

Syphilis: The Great Imitator

In 1492, Christopher Columbus's sailors became infected with syphilis in the Americas and carried the disease back to Europe. It quickly spread throughout the continent, destroying hundreds of thousands of lives. The syphilis epidemic in Europe would persist for several hundred years. Doctors usually treated the disease with mercury, a treatment that often caused the death of the patients. Today, penicillin or certain other antibiotics are used to treat syphilis. The antibiotics can cure the disease. You can be reinfected with syphilis after having been cured, because the body does not build up an immunity to it.

Syphilis is caused by a bacterium called *Treponema pallidum.* The syphilis bacteria is spread through direct contact between a syphilis sore and the moist lining of the genitals, mouth, or anus of a sexual partner. You can protect yourself against syphilis infection by making sure you use a condom during vaginal, oral, or anal sex.

More than fifty thousand people are diagnosed with syphilis each year in the United States. The progression of the disease follows a complex course, consisting of three stages. Antibiotics can cure syphilis at any stage. However, antibiotics cannot repair

A poster from 1938 urges people to be tested for syphilis infection. The disease, which spread throughout Europe after 1500, can be cured with antibiotics.

damage to the internal organs during the third stage of the disease. Syphilis is known as the "great imitator," because its early symptoms can be confused with those of other diseases. For several hundred years, syphilis was believed to be an especially virulent form of gonorrhea.

When a person first gets syphilis, he or she will typically develop a small sore ten to ninety days after becoming infected. The sore will appear inside the vagina, near the tip of the penis, or even in the mouth or anus. The sores usually ooze fluid. Some people may not realize they are infected, since the sores are usually painless. If left untreated, the sore will eventually disappear by itself within one to five weeks. The reason syphilis is so dangerous is that infected people at this point may believe they are cured. Unfortunately this is not the case, and the syphilis bacteria are instead progressing to stage two.

During stage two, the infected person will break out in a rash. This usually occurs within weeks or months after the initial sore disappears. The rash appears on the palms of the hands, the soles of the feet, or other parts of the body. It usually consists of rough, reddish-brown spots, but it can also resemble a heat rash. The infected person also often suffers from flulike symptoms. The fever, aches, and swollen glands may come and go for as long as two years. Finally the symptoms stop. Once again, unless they have been treated for the disease, some people may be tempted to believe they are cured. However, the bacteria remain in the body, though they are no longer infectious. The bacteria will now remain dormant for a long time, sometimes up to forty years.

About two thirds of infected people will never experience any further symptoms, but the other third are in serious trouble. Indeed, the syphilis bacteria are now a threat to the infected person's life. Stage three syphilis progresses over a period of years. When the syphilis bacteria become active once again in stage three, they can damage the internal organs and nervous system. Symptoms vary from one person to another. They include heart disease leading to heart failure, nerve damage leading to paralysis, brain damage leading to insanity, blindness, bone and joint damage, and chronic vomiting and abdominal pain.

People diagnosed with syphilis should be tested for other STDs as well. If you have had sex with a person infected with syphilis within ninety days of that person being diagnosed, you should be treated, whether or not you have symptoms. Syphilis is reportable to the health department in most states. There are anonymous partner notification programs so that persons who may have been infected can be called in for treatment.

The Most Dangerous STD: HIV and AIDS

AIDS (acquired immunodeficiency syndrome) is a very complex sexually transmitted disease caused by the human immunodeficiency virus (HIV). HIV is a retrovirus that destroys the immune system. The immune system produces lymphocytes, white blood cells that destroy cancer cells and pathogens such as bacteria, viruses, and fungi. When the immune system is weakened or destroyed, the body can no longer fight disease. The HIV retrovirus targets two types of lymphocytes, the T-helper and T-suppressor cells. These T cells regulate the immune system by controlling the strength and quality of all immune responses.

Most healthy people have between 500 and 1,600 T cells. When HIV infects the body, the number of T cells goes down as the virus circulates in the system. For a time, the body is strong enough to resist the action of the virus. Eventually, however, the immune system becomes seriously impaired. When the T cell count falls below 200, the person is now considered to have AIDS. He or she is now at high risk of developing a variety of infections and diseases that will eventually result in death.

The first reports of people dying from AIDS emerged in the early 1980s. The understanding that HIV was the cause of AIDS came soon after. Lisa Marr notes: "Worldwide, more than twenty-five million people have died in the AIDS epidemic, and more than forty million people are thought to be infected with HIV.... In the United States, more than 700,000 people are infected, and more than 450,000 have died since 1981."[15]

In the United States, it used to be that homosexual men were the main group of people infected with HIV. But recently, the level of infection among women and teens has risen. According to the U.S. Department of Health and Human Services, "In 2006, young adults aged 13 to 29 accounted for the largest number of new HIV infections in the United States.... The rate of HIV among young women aged 16 to 21 is 50 percent higher than the rate among young men in that age group."[16]

HIV can be spread three ways—sexual transmission, contact with infected blood, and transmission from mother to child. Sexual transmission includes unprotected vaginal, anal, or oral sex. Obviously, safer sex—using a condom—is essential to protect

World AIDS Day

On December 1 each year, people all around the world show their commitment to raising awareness about HIV and AIDS by wearing red ribbons. Indeed, many wear a red ribbon all year round. The red ribbon has become a symbol for solidarity with HIV-positive people and those living with AIDS.

In 1987, James W. Bunn and Thomas Netter came up with the idea of World AIDS Day. The two men worked as public information officers for the Global Programme on AIDS (now known as UNAIDS) at the World Health Organization. They had been looking for an effective way to attract the world's attention to the tragic predicament of the millions of people around the globe suffering from HIV and AIDS. The first World AIDS Day occurred on December 1, 1988.

The current theme of World AIDS day is "Stop AIDS. Keep the promise." World AIDS Day activities are focused on raising money, increasing awareness, fighting prejudice, and improving education. On this day, memorials are held to honor those who have died from HIV/AIDS. Government and health officials give speeches on AIDS topics. World AIDS Day reminds people that HIV has not gone away and that there are many things still to be done.

Students take part in a candlelight vigil to raise awareness of HIV/AIDS. Medical advances in recent years offer some hope to those with AIDS, but there is currently no cure or preventive vaccine.

against exposure to the HIV retrovirus. Contact with infected blood can occur through an exchange of needles related to intravenous drug abuse or through body piercing or tattooing. Transmission from mother to fetus can occur during pregnancy and from mother to baby during childbirth or breastfeeding.

There has been a great deal of misinformation about HIV, especially during the early years of the AIDS epidemic. This led to needless suffering on the part of people with AIDS, who were sometimes abandoned because of unfounded fears. People infected with HIV were denied access to insurance and health care, lost jobs and housing, became targets of social stigma, and were often blamed for their illness—at least in part because HIV was frequently contracted through activities not approved of by society, such as drug use or gay sex. Before much was known about HIV/AIDS, many people did not understand that a person cannot get the virus by kissing, hugging, or sharing food with someone with HIV. Nor can HIV be transmitted by sneezing, coughing, or breathing on food. You cannot get HIV by donating blood. (Fears about the blood supply arose in the early days of the epidemic, when people contracted HIV after receiving transfusions with tainted blood; however, blood is routinely tested now and is safe.)

Many people infected with HIV have no symptoms. They feel fine and look fine. Indeed, they would not know they were infected unless they were tested. Newly infected people often develop a flulike illness within two to six weeks of becoming infected. Symptoms include a sore throat,

HIV can be spread three ways— sexual transmission, contact with infected blood, and transmission from mother to child.

fever, night sweats, lymph node swelling throughout the body, muscle aches, and a flat, red rash over the entire body. Women with HIV may also get severe vaginal infections and pelvic inflammatory disease. These symptoms, which usually last one or two weeks, go away on their own.

After the initial infection, a person may go quite a while—sometimes as long as ten years—without symptoms. Then, as the immune system grows weaker, people with AIDS become seriously ill with what are called opportunistic infections. They may develop pneumonia; severe diarrhea, vomiting, or stomach cramps; severe headaches; problems with eyesight and eventually blindness; confusion, forgetfulness, and loss of coordination; and certain cancers, especially a skin cancer called Kaposi's sarcoma. Eventually, people with AIDS die from one of their infections.

There is no cure for HIV, but there are now drugs available that allow people infected with HIV/AIDS to live longer and healthier lives. These drugs are expensive, they can have many side effects, and they cannot cure people. Most people infected with HIV eventually die from AIDS-related causes, although life expectancy is increasing due to new medications.

Today, sex education in America's schools is pretty close to universal for young people. Almost all students in the United States receive some form of sex education at least once between grades seven and twelve.[1] In many schools, some topics in sex education are taught as early as grades five or six. In some schools, even younger students are introduced to certain topics, such as "stranger danger," to protect them from sexual predators.

Back in 1967, during the early days of the sexual revolution, the Illinois Sex Education Advisory Board came up with guidelines for sex education that became a model for such programs. The board members took into account the new challenges for teenagers brought about by the changes in sexual behavior. According to their recommendations:

> Provision should be made for class discussion and communication among students, teachers, and counselors, which will guide and assist Illinois youth in critically and constructively analyzing current sexual problems and issues and in drawing sound conclusions, desirable from both a personal and a social standpoint. We must have faith that when young people in Illinois are given the facts and then guided in thinking things through, the vast majority will choose the right path instead of the wrong.[2]

Should Sex Education Be Provided in Schools?

During the decades since the sexual revolution of the 1960s, a division has widened between those who hold liberal sexual values and those who hold conservative ones. The liberal approach favors comprehensive sex education. Conservatives oppose such sex education and support abstinence-only sex education. Among the conservatives is a small but vocal minority whose members oppose all sex education in the schools. They believe that parents should be the ones solely responsible for their children's education about sex. They think that sex education in the schools represents government interference by encouraging such immoral practices as premarital sex and homosexuality.

One conservative school board member said to the health curriculum committee:

> My children were outside in the snow, sled riding. And we're talking about nine-, ten-, eight-, eleven-, twelve-year-olds. All they did all day was slide up and down that hill, up and down that hill. Do you think for one minute they had the thought of sex on their minds, or condoms or spermicide? No, that's not in their world right now. And why should we be forcing them? Why should we put that burden on them? You know, I think that's wrong. I see it as child abuse, I really do.[3]

Eleanor Howe, a conservative who is proud of shutting down the sex education program in Anaheim, California, said:

I've been vindicated. I made the statement at a school-board meeting that if they continued with this type of sex instruction—I never called it education—that they were going to find it necessary to distribute condoms and other birth-control devices in our junior-high schools, and everybody laughed. They just thought that was the funniest thing. And yet that's precisely what they're doing now.... That's how far this whole thing has gone toward changing the values of an entire society. That's what I foresaw, and now all I can say is, "I told you so some twenty-some years ago."[4]

While some people object to sex education in schools, the vast majority of American parents support school sex education programs. According to a survey conducted by the organizations Advocates for Youth and the Sexuality Information and Education Council of the United States (SIECUS), 93 percent of Americans support the teaching of sexuality education in high schools, while 84 percent support it in middle and junior high schools.[5]

Mary Calderone

Mary Calderone (1904–1998) was a pioneer in the field of human sexuality. She became an outspoken advocate for sex education at a time when sex was not discussed in public. According to Calderone, "We're still a sexophobic society, afraid of the wrong things for the wrong reason."[6] She believed that birth control, medical information, and treatment for sexually transmitted diseases should be available to everyone. She also believed that children should learn the basic facts about sexuality as early as kindergarten.

As a child, Calderone grew up around art. Her father was the famous photographer Edward Steichen, and her uncle was the poet Carl Sandburg. After graduating from college, Calderone pursued a stage career for several years. She then went back to school and studied medicine, getting an MD degree in 1939.

In 1953, Calderone became medical director of the Planned Parenthood Federation of America. She became known for her strenuous efforts at giving out information about birth control and campaigning for the legalization of abortion. In 1964, Calderone, after repeated appeals, persuaded the American Medical Association (AMA) to repeal its rule prohibiting doctors from providing birth control information. Also in 1964, she became cofounder of the Sex Information and Education Council of the United States (SIECUS).

Most teens say they would prefer to get information about sex from their parents, but in most families there is a lack of such parent-teen communication. According to one report, "Fewer than 20 percent of the parents were a major source of information regarding sexuality education." Another report in 1998 found that "between 30 and 40 percent of high school students had had 'one good talk' with their parents—almost always their mother—about STDs and whether teen sex was 'okay.'"[7]

Abstinence-Only Sex Education

Most Americans support sex education programs in the schools. But for years there has been heated debate between conservatives, who favor abstinence-only programs, and liberals, who are in favor of comprehensive programs. Conservatives tend to believe that comprehensive sex education is to blame for the soaring rates of teen pregnancy and sexually transmitted disease. Liberals, on the other hand, believe that it is the absence of comprehensive sex education that is responsible for the rise in teen pregnancy and STDs.

Some abstinence-only programs tend to confuse values with health. Their students read textbooks filled with catchy slogans such as "Don't be a louse, wait for your spouse!" "Do the right thing, wait for the ring!" and "Pet your dog, not your date!" Some of these teachers have been telling their students that birth control does not avert pregnancy among teenagers and that condoms fail to protect against sexually transmitted diseases. They mislead young people when they tell them that all sexual activity outside marriage is harmful and that only abstinence will protect them. According to its critics, abstinence-only sex education is in direct conflict with science and ignores the overwhelming evidence that other programs are more effective. There has been no evidence that abstinence-only programs are better than comprehensive programs at preventing teen pregnancy and STDs.[8]

The Alabama state health department runs an educational program that stresses abstinence before marriage. Such programs have recently come under attack as being ineffective and confusing values with health.

A school district nurse presents a unit on birth control and STDs in Yakima, Washington. While the vast majority of adults believe that abstinence should be included in sex education programs, most believe teaching abstinence alone is not enough.

Not surprisingly, liberals seem to be winning the argument. According to Advocates for Youth, at least 69 percent of Americans agree that teaching abstinence-only-until-marriage is not realistic. More than 90 percent of adults support including abstinence as a topic in comprehensive sexuality education in high school. But 70 percent oppose the provision of federal law that allocates over half a billion tax dollars for abstinence-only-until-marriage education but prohibits use of the funds for teaching about the use of condoms and contraception for the prevention of unintended pregnancy and STDs.[9]

In what appears to be a trend, states and school districts are turning away from abstinence-only sex education programs, presumably because of poor results. In December 2007, fourteen states notified the federal government that they would no longer be seeking money for abstinence-only programs.[10]

Writer Kristin Luker finds some value in programs that promote abstinence only. According to Luker, such programs help teens resist strong peer pressure to engage in sex. She believes that

> abstinence programs may in fact provide valuable social support for the idea that young people (young women in particular) don't have to be sexually active if they don't want to be.... Most comprehensive sex education programs include units that teach students how to reject sexual advances they are not comfortable with, but the passion and fervor that abstinence advocates bring to their cause puts some real muscle into those teachings.[11]

Sex Education Programs

Advocates for Youth presents the following point-by-point comparison of comprehensive sex education programs and programs that teach abstinence only until marriage. The guidelines and content represent the typical material included in the two kinds of courses.

Comprehensive Sex Education

1. Teaches that sexuality is a natural, normal, healthy part of life.

2. Teaches that abstinence from sexual intercourse is the most effective method of preventing unintended pregnancy and sexually transmitted diseases, including HIV.

3. Provides values-based education and offers students the opportunity to explore and define their individual values as well as the values of their families and communities.

4. Includes a wide variety of sexuality related topics, such as human development, relationships, interpersonal skills, sexual expression, sexual health, and society and culture.

5. Includes accurate, factual information on abortion, masturbation, and sexual orientation.

6. Provides positive messages about sexuality and sexual expression, including the benefits of abstinence.

7. Teaches that proper use of latex condoms can greatly reduce, but not eliminate, the risk of unintended pregnancy and sexually transmitted infections, including HIV.

8. Teaches that consistent use of modern methods of contraception can greatly reduce a couple's risk for unintended pregnancy.

9. Includes accurate medical information about STDs, including HIV; teaches that individuals can avoid STDs.

10. Teaches that religious values can play an important role in an individual's decisions about sexual expression; offers students the opportunity to explore their own and their family's religious values.

11. Teaches that a woman faced with an unintended pregnancy has options: carrying the pregnancy to term and raising the baby, carrying the pregnancy to term and placing the baby for adoption, or ending the pregnancy with an abortion.

Young people need to be informed so that they can make responsible, healthy decisions about their sexual lives.

Abstinence-Only-Until-Marriage Education

1. Teaches that sexual expression outside of marriage will have harmful social, psychological, and physical consequences.

2. Teaches that sexual abstinence before marriage is the only acceptable behavior.

3. Teaches only one set of values as morally correct for all students.

4. Limits topics to abstinence-only-until-marriage and to the negative consequences of premarital sexual activity.

5. Usually omits controversial topics such as abortion, sexual orientation, and masturbation.

6. Often uses fear tactics to promote abstinence and to limit sexual expression.

7. Discusses condoms only in terms of failure rates; often exaggerates condom failure rates.

8. Provides no information on forms of contraception other than failure rates of condoms and contraception.

9. Often includes inaccurate information and exaggerated statistics regarding STDs, including HIV; suggests that STDs are an inevitable result of premarital sexual behavior.

10. Often promotes specific religious values.

11. Teaches that carrying the pregnancy to term and either placing the baby for adoption or getting married and keeping the baby are the only morally correct options for pregnant teens.[12]

Sex education is an important part of your school career. It is up to you to learn to make healthy, responsible decisions about your sexuality. Life is uncertain, and sex, like many other things in life, is not without risks. What you can control is how you act. Love yourself enough to be sexually smart. You owe it to yourself to feel good about yourself and your body, remain healthy, and build positive, loving relationships.

Chapter Notes

Chapter 1 Teen Sexual Behavior

1. Kristin Luker, *When Sex Goes to School* (New York: W. W. Norton & Company, 2006), p. 69.

2. Tom Wolfe, *Hooking Up* (New York: Farrar, Straus, Giroux), 2000.

3. Sabrina Weill, *The Real Truth About Teens & Sex* (New York: The Berkley Publishing Group, 2005), p. 112.

4. Kristin Luker, *Dubious Conceptions: The Politics of Teenage Pregnancy* (Cambridge, Mass: Harvard University Press, 1996), p. 91.

5. "The 'Talk," *WebMD,* November 26, 2001, <http://www.webmd.com/sex-relationships/features/ broaching-birds-bees> (December 19, 2008).

6. Judith Levine, *Harmful to Minors: The Perils of Protecting Children from Sex* (Minneapolis: University of Minnesota Press, 2002), p. xxvi.

7. Weill, p. 111.

8. Lynn Elber, "TV Teaches Teenagers About Sex—Media Project Teaches TV," Associated Press, December 26, 2002, <http://www.aegis.com/news/ads/2002/ad022489.html> (December 19, 2008).

9. Kathleen A. Bogle, *Hooking Up: Sex, Dating, and Relationships on Campus* (New York: New York University Press, 2008), p. 2.

10. Ibid.

11. Eric Marcus, *Is It a Choice?* (New York: HarperCollins Publishers, 1999), p. 41.

12. Ibid., p. 11.

13. Marilyn Elias, "Gay Teens Coming Out Earlier to Peers and Family," *USA Today,* February 7, 2007, <http://www.usatoday.

com/news/nation/2007-02-07-gay-teens-cover_x.htm>
(December 19, 2008).

14. Ritch C. Savin-Williams, *The New Gay Teenager*
    (Cambridge, Mass.: Harvard University Press, 2005), p. 1.

15. Carol Platt Liebau, *Prude* (New York: Hachette Book
    Group USA, 2007), p. 32.

16. "Our Mission," GLSEN, n.d., <http://www.glsen.org/
    cgi-bin/iowa/all/about/history/index.html> (December 23,
    2008).

Chapter 2 Birth Control

1. "Facts on Contraceptive Use," Guttmacher Institute,
    January 2008, <http://www.guttmacher.org/
    pubs/fb_contr_use.html> (November 20, 2008).

2. Ibid.

3. Kristin Luker, *Dubious Conceptions: The Politics of Teenage
    Pregnancy* (Cambridge, Mass.: Harvard University Press,
    1996), p. 93.

4. Ibid., pp. 94–95.

5. "Facts on Contraceptive Use."

6. Ibid.

7. Ibid.

8. Ibid.

9. Ibid.

10. Ibid.

11. Amy G. Miron and Charles D. Miron, *How to Talk with
    Teens About Love, Relationships, & S-E-X: A Guide for
    Parents* (Minneapolis: Free Spirit Publishing, Inc., 2002),
    p. 197.

Chapter 3 Teen Pregnancy

1. Bob Herbert, "A Dubious Milestone," *New York Times,* June 21, 2008, <http://www.nytimes.com/2008/06/21/opinion/21 herbert.html?hp> (October 17, 2008).

2. Ruth Sidel, *Unsung Heroines* (Berkeley: University of California Press, 2006), p. 188.

3. "Why It Matters: Teen Pregnancy and Education," The National Campaign to Prevent Unwanted and Teen Pregnancy, n.d., <http://www.thenationalcampaign.org/why-it-matters/pdf/education.pdf> (November 20, 2008).

4. "Why It Matters: Teen Pregnancy, Poverty, and Income Disparity," The National Campaign to Prevent Unwanted and Teen Pregnancy, n.d., <http://www.thenationalcampaign.org/why-it-matters/pdf/poverty.pdf> (November 20, 2008).

5. Ibid.

6. Sidel, p. 189.

7. Lynn Ponton, "The Sex Lives of Teenagers," *Reality Check: Teen Pregnancy Prevention Strategies That Work* (Get Real About Teen Pregnancy Campaign, 2004), p. 141.

8. Sidel, p. 189.

9. R. F. Blader, "It's Not About Sex: The Politics of Teen Pregnancy," *Counterpunch* newsletter, December 18, 2007, <http://www.counterpunch.org/blader12181007.html> (October 17, 2008).

10. Jennifer C. Kerr, "Report: Teen birth rate hits record low," *USA Today,* July 16, 2007, <http://www.usatoday.com/news/health/2007-07-16-3524503849_x.htm> (November 20, 2008).

11. Ibid.

12. "In Brief: Fact on American Teens' Sexual and Reproductive Health," Guttmacher Institute, September 2006, <http://www.guttmacher.org/pubs/fb_ATSRH.html> (November 25, 2008).

13. Ibid.

14. William H. Honan, "Honor Society Ordered to Admit Pregnant Girls," *New York Times,* December 30, 1998, <http://query.nytimes.com/gst/fullpage.html?res=9E05EF D8123FF933A05751C1A96E958260> (November 21, 2008); "'Disparate Impact' Acknowledged in Discrimination Against Pregnant Students' Membership in the National Honor Society," Feminist Majority Foundation, 2007, <http://www.feminist.org/education/consequences.asp> (November 21, 2008).

15. Kay S. Hymowitz, "There's No Honor in Unwed Motherhood," *The Wall Street Journal,* August 12, 1998, <http://www.manhattan-institute.org/html/_wsj-theres_no_honor.htm> (November 21, 2008).

Chapter 4 Sexually Transmitted Diseases

1. Sabrina Weill, *The Real Truth About Teens & Sex* (New York: The Berkley Publishing Group, 2005), p. 183.

2. Leonard Pitts, Jr., "Abstinence-Only Policy Is Bearing Fruit," *Miami Herald,* June 25, 2008.

3. David B. Caruso, "NYC urges docs to do routine HIV testing on adults," Associated Press, June 2008.

4. Lisa Marr, *Sexually Transmitted Diseases: A Physician Tells You What You Need to Know* (Baltimore: The Johns Hopkins University Press, 2007), p. 211.

5. Ibid., p. 171.

6. Ibid., p. 153.

7. Miranda Hitti, "Gardasil Approved to Target More Cancers: FDA Expands HPV Vaccine Gardasil to Prevent

Certain Cancers of the Vulva and Vagina," *WebMD Health News,* September 12, 2008, <http://children. webmd.com/vaccines/news/20080912/gardasil-approved-to-treat-more-cancers> (December 22, 2008).

8. "Human Papillomavirus (HPV) Vaccine: What You Need to Know," *WebMD Children's Vaccines Health Center,* n.d., <http://webmd.com/vaccines/hpv-vaccine-what-you-need-know> (December 22, 2008).

9. Erin Allday, "UCSF doctors warn on wide use of cervical cancer vaccine," *San Francisco Chronicle,* May 10, 2007.

10. Karen Houppert, "Who's Afraid of Gardasil?" *The Nation,* March 26, 2007, p. 20.

11. Ibid.

12. Ibid.

13. Paige Bierma, "Gonorrhea," Consumer Health Interactive, April 27, 2009, <http://www.ahealthyme.com/topic/topic13106> (May 6, 2009).

14. "Gonorrhea," Planned Parenthood, March 23, 2008, <http://www.plannedparenthood.org;health-topics/stds-hiv-safer-sex/gonorrhea-4269.htm> (May 6, 2009).

15. Marr, p. 245.

16. "Women and HIV/AIDS," U.S. Department of Health and Human Services, n.d., <http://www.womenshealth.gov/hiv/women-at-risk> (June 11, 2009).

Chapter 5 Sex Education in Schools

1. David J. Landry, Susheela Singh, and Jacqueline E. Darroch, "Sexuality Education in Fifth and Sixth Grades in U.S. Public Schools, 1999," *Family Planning Perspectives,* 32(5), September/October 2000, <http://www.guttmacher.org/pubs/journals/3221200.html> (November 21, 2008).

2. Kristin Luker, *When Sex Goes to School* (New York: W. W. Norton & Company, 2006), pp. 84–85.

3. Janice M. Irvine, *Talk About Sex: The Battles over Sex Education in the United States* (Berkeley, Calif.: University of California Press, 2002, p. 139.

4. Ibid., p. 61.

5. "Americans Support Sexuality Education, Including Information on Abstinence and Contraception," Advocates for Youth, n.d., <http://www.advocatesforyouth.org/facts-figures/suppsexed.htm> (November 25, 2008).

6. "Mary Calderone," *Columbia 250*, 2004, <http://www.c250.columbia.edu/c250_celebrates/remarkable_columbians/mary_calderone.html> (May 4, 2009).

7. Jeffrey P. Moran, *Teaching Sex: The Shaping of Adolescence in the 20th Century* (Cambridge, Mass.: Harvard University Press, 2000), p. 227.

8. "In Brief: Facts on Sex Education in the United States," Guttmacher Institute, December 2006, <http://www.guttmacher.org/pubs/fb_sexEd2006.html> (November 25, 2008).

9. "Americans Support Sexuality Education, Including Information on Abstinence and Contraception."

10. "In Sex Ed, Abstinence-Only Loses Support but Keeps Funds," *USA Today: Opinion,* December 26, 2007, <http://blogs.usatoday.com/oped/2007/12/in-sex-ed-absti.html> (November 25, 2008).

11. Luker, p. 257.

12. "Sex Education Programs: Definitions and Point-by-Point Comparison," Advocates for Youth, May 2008, <http://www.advocatesforyouth.org/rrr/definitions.htm> (November 25, 2008).

Glossary

abortion—The termination, or ending, of a pregnancy.

abstinence—The state of not being sexually active.

AIDS—Acquired immunodeficiency syndrome, a suppression of the body's immune system caused by the HIV virus, which leaves the body unable to fight infections. Currently, there is no cure.

anal sex—The insertion of a penis or object into the anus of another person.

bacteria—Microscopic organisms that may cause disease. Antibiotics are used to fight bacteria.

birth control—Various ways to prevent pregnancy. Also called contraception.

birth control pills—An oral prescription method of birth control, consisting of pills containing the hormones estrogen and progestin or progestin alone. Also called "the pill."

bisexual—A person who is romantically and sexually attracted to both men and women.

casual sex—Sexual behavior engaged in without a long-term commitment to a relationship.

chlamydia—The most common sexually transmitted bacterial infection in the United States.

condom—A thin protective covering made from latex that is placed over an erect penis to prevent sperm from entering the vagina and to protect against the spread of STDs.

ejaculation—The muscular contractions that quickly move sperm and semen out of the penis.

erection—The stiffening and enlargement of the penis, usually a response to sexual arousal.

fallopian tubes—Two narrow tubes connected to the top of the uterus that form a pathway for an ovum, or egg, to travel from the ovary to the uterus.

female condom—A polyurethane pouch with flexible rings at both ends that is inserted into the vagina to protect against pregnancy and STDs.

fertilization—The penetration of the egg by a sperm, which results in conception.

Gardasil—A vaccine that can protect girls against certain strains of human papillomavirus (HPV).

gay—A widely used term for homosexual.

gender—Whether a person is male or female.

gonorrhea—A sexually transmitted disease caused by a bacteria; also known as "the clap."

herpes—Caused by the herpes simplex virus (HSV). It causes painful blisters and is spread by skin-to-skin contact with an infected area.

heterosexual—A person who is romantically and sexually attracted to people of the other sex.

homosexual—A person who is romantically and sexually attracted to people of the same sex.

hormones—Chemical substances secreted directly into the bloodstream. Hormones such as estrogen, progesterone, and testosterone affect sexuality and reproduction.

human immunodeficiency virus (HIV)—A virus that attacks the body's immune system and gradually leaves the infected person unable to fight off infections and diseases; eventually develops into AIDS, which has no known cure.

human papillomavirus (HPV)— A virus that results in very contagious genital warts and can also cause cervical cancer.

intercourse—Sexual activity involving the insertion of a man's penis into a woman's vagina.

intrauterine device—A plastic or metal device inserted into the uterus by a health care professional to prevent pregnancy; commonly known as an IUD.

lesbian—A woman who is romantically and sexually attracted to other women.

monogamous—Having only one sexual or marital partner at a time.

opportunistic infections—Infections caused by usually harmless microorganisms that can cause disease when a person's resistance is impaired.

oral sex—Sexual stimulation of the genitals or anus by the mouth.

orgasm—The peak of sexual excitement, usually achieved by stimulation of the genitals. It results in involuntary contraction of pelvic muscles and ejaculation in males.

ovaries—The two gonads, or sex glands, of the female. They contain eggs and produce the female hormones estrogen and progesterone.

ovulation—The release of a mature ovum from the ovaries.

Pap smear—A common medical test that examines cervical cells to see if they are normal or abnormal (leading to cancer or cancerous). Also called a Pap smear.

pelvic inflammatory disease (PID)—Infection in the uterus or pelvic area, usually caused by a sexually transmitted infection.

penis—The external male sexual organ, which becomes erect when sexually excited.

safer sex—Various behaviors that minimize the possibility of exchanging body fluids and, therefore, help protect against pregnancy and STDs.

sexually transmitted disease (STD)—Any one of a group of diseases, infections, and parasites that are passed from one person to another through sexual contact. Also called STI (sexually transmitted infection).

sperm—The reproductive sex cell of a man that is produced in the testicles and ejaculated out of the penis in semen.

syphilis—A sexually transmitted disease caused by bacteria.

trichomoniasis—A sexually transmitted disease caused by a parasite. Also called "trich."

uterus—The organ in a woman that holds and nurtures a developing baby. Also known as the womb.

vagina—The pathway between the outside of the body and the cervix. A baby passes through the vagina during a normal birth; the penis is inserted into the vagina during sexual intercourse.

virus—An organism that invades a cell and uses the cell to create more viral material.

For More Information

Advocates for Youth
> (202) 347-5700
> Provides information on sexual health, sexual orientation, and links to helping organizations.

American Social Health Association
> (919) 361-8400
> Provides facts, support, and resources so people can find referrals, join support groups, and get access to in-depth information about sexually transmitted infections, including HPV.

National STD Hotline
> 1-800-227-8922
> Provides information about STDs and sexual health for teens.

Centers for Disease Control and Prevention
> STD Hotline and HIV/AIDS Hotline: 1-800-232-4636
> Traveler's Health Hotline: 1-877-394-8747

GLSEN (Gay, Lesbian and Straight Education Network)
> (212) 727-0135
> Provides lesson plans for educator training programs and activities, suggestions to make campus GSAs more inclusive, and a diverse collection of resources and support for educators and students to empower them to make their schools safe for all students, regardless of sexual orientation or gender identity/expression.

Henry J. Kaiser Family Foundation
> (650) 854-9400
> Provides facts and analysis on major health care issues for policymakers, the media, the health care community, and the general public.

Herpes Resource Center
(American Social Health Association)
(604) 299-1171
Provides up-to-date information on herpes blood testing, location of herpes support groups, online chat room on herpes, and literature about herpes and other STDs.

National Abortion Federation
1-800-772-9100
Provides confidential information on pregnancy and abortion along with local referrals.

National Adoption Information Clearinghouse
1-888-251-0075
Provides professionals and the general public with information on all aspects of adoption, including infant and intercountry adoption and the adoption of children with special needs.

National Campaign to Prevent Teen and Uplanned Pregnancy
(202) 478-8500
Provides useful information for parents and teens.

PFLAG (Parents, Families and Friends of Lesbians and Gays)
(202) 467-8180
Provides opportunity for dialogue about sexual orientation and gender identity, and acts to create a society that is healthy and respectful of human diversity.

Planned Parenthood Federation of America
1-800-230-PLAN
Planned Parenthood is often the best source of information, contraception, and emergency services for teens and young adults.

Sexuality Information and Education Council of the
United States (SIECUS)
(212) 819-9770
The nation's best-known advocate for sex education. SIECUS provides information, promotes comprehensive education about sexuality, and advocates the right of individuals to make responsible sexual choices.

Further Reading

Books

Corinna, Heather. *S.E.X..: The All-You-Need-to-Know Progressive Sexuality Guide to Get You Through High School and College.* New York: Marlowe & Company, 2007.

Gowen, L. Kris. *Sexual Decisions.* Blue Ridge Summit, Pa.: Scarecrow Trade/National Book Network, 2007.

Hyde, Margaret O., and Elizabeth H. Forsyth. *Safe Sex 101: An Overview for Teens.* Minneapolis, Minn.: Twenty-First Century Books, 2006.

Pardes, Bronwen. *Doing It Right: Making Smart, Safe, and Satisfying Choices About Sex.* New York: Simon & Schuster, 2007.

Wells, Ken R., ed. *Teenage Sexuality: Opposing Viewpoints.* Farmington Hills, Mich.: Greenhaven Press/Thomson Gale, 2006.

Internet Addresses

Sexuality Information and Education Council of the United States (SIECUS)
<http://www.siecus.org/pubs/fact/fact0007.html>

Teen Talk for information about sexuality and relationships from Planned Parenthood
<http://www.plannedparenthood.org/teen-talk/index.htm>

Index

FEB 1 5 2011